MW01076441

BEGINNER THEORY FOR CHILDREN

BOOK THREE

BILL'S MUSIC SHELF

BY MELANIE SMITH

Visit us on the Web at www.melbay.com or billsmusicshelf.com

FOREWORD

In creating this workbook, I have relied on my educational experience and many years of violin as a basis for this style of instruction. With a degree in psychology, an after degree in elementary education and a masters degree in music education, I have used techniques to teach children effectively while still keeping it fun — the major emphasis of learning violin at an early age. This book is designed to teach theory at a level that is attainable, yet challenging. It is intended to build confidence and solidify the relationship between theory and playing. It is written so it can be used to teach beginners the basics of theory, or even to refresh musicians who might need a small review. No matter who uses this book, it will give a strong foundation to violin and, through this understanding, will foster a greater love of playing.

TABLE OF CONTENTS

DRAWING SHARPS

When drawing sharps, make sure the middle of the sharp is on a space or line.

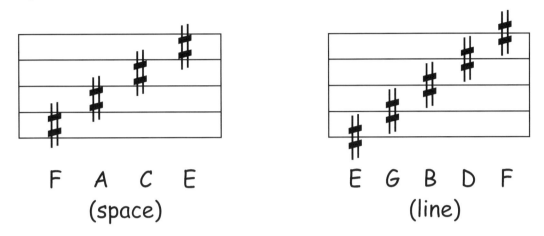

F   A   C   E
(space)

E G B D F
(line)

Write the name of the sharp in the box below. Look carefully to see if the sharp is on a space or line.

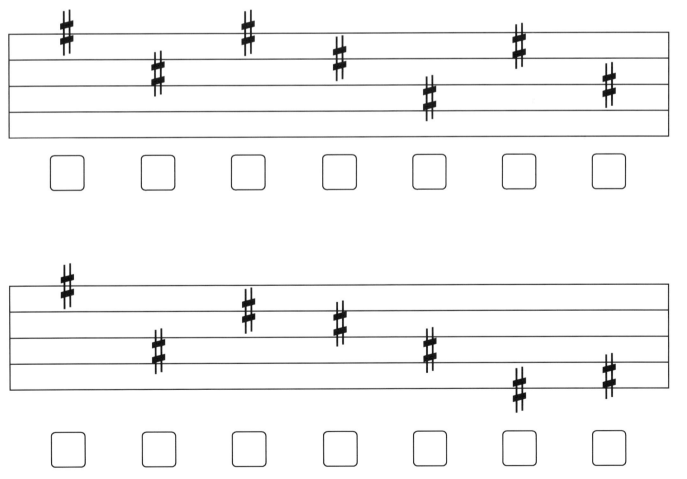

1

Write the name of the sharp in the box below. Look carefully to see if the sharp is on a space or line.

Use the sharp name below to draw the sharp on the space or line where it belongs.

F C A B E D F

A C E D B C A

B A B D C E F

D F A C A B D

3

Use the sharp name below to draw the sharp on the space or
line where it belongs.

| B | A | E | D | F | B | C |

| C | E | F | D | A | D | F |

| F | A | C | E | F | D | B |

| A | B | F | D | A | B | E |

4

Draw sharps on the music staff using the words below.

D   A   D

D   E   E   D

B   E   G

D   E   A   D

B   E   E   F

B   A   G

A   C   E

A   D   D

5

Fill in the boxes and find out what words appear using the sharps below.

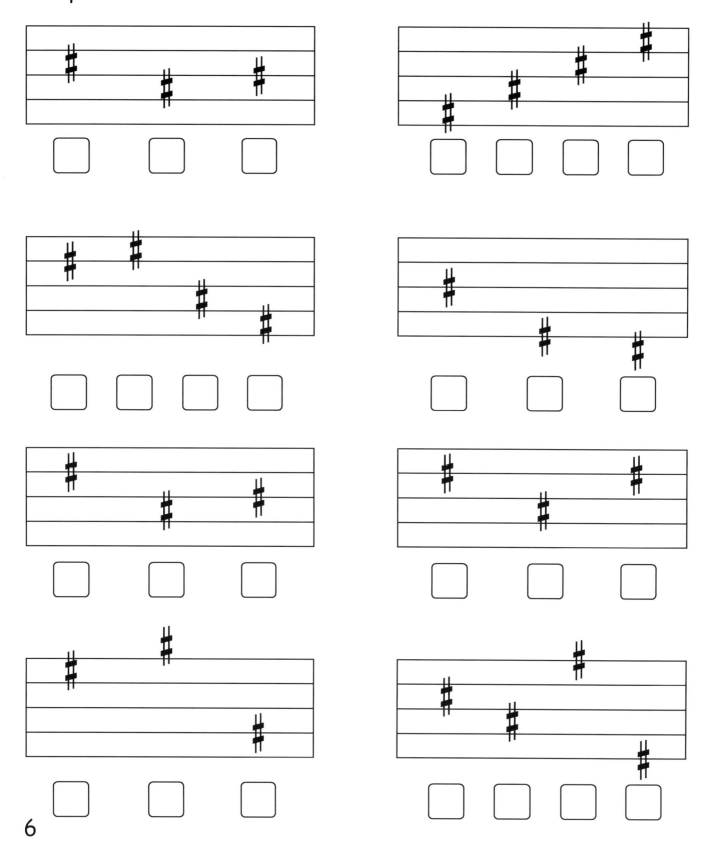

6

ORDER OF SHARPS

Written music has seven sharps which are always placed after the treble clef.

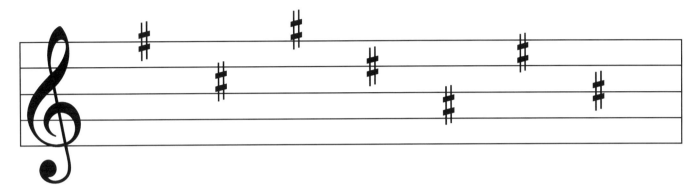

Each of these sharps are on a specific space or line and are always in this order.

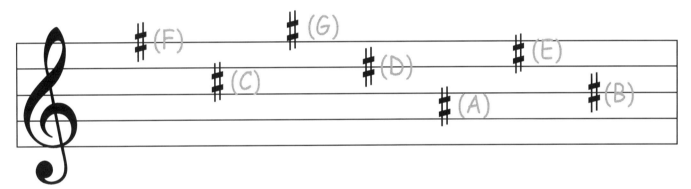

Here is an easy way to remember them. Use this saying:

Father Charles Goes Down And Ends Battle
1   2   3   4   5   6   7

What are the seven sharps? List from left to right.

____ ____ ____ ____ ____ ____ ____

Write the names of the seven sharps in order using the boxes below.
Here is an example.

Draw the seven sharps in the correct order and write their names underneath.

LEARNING KEY SIGNATURES WITH SHARPS

Key signatures are important because they let you know where to put your fingers on the violin. Key signatures are always written after the treble clef.

Here are **4** important sharp key signatures you should know.

A Major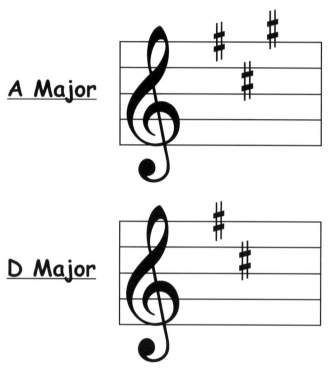

The key of A major has 3 sharps.

$$F^\sharp, C^\sharp, \text{ and } G^\sharp$$

D Major

The key of D major has 2 sharps.

$$F^\sharp \text{ and } C^\sharp$$

G Major

The key of G major has 1 sharp.

$$F^\sharp$$

C Major

The key of C major has zero sharps.

DRAWING KEY SIGNATURES WITH SHARPS

To draw key signatures with sharps, you will need to remember the saying you learned earlier. For this exercise, draw the correct number of sharps in each key signature and write the letter name of each sharp underneath.

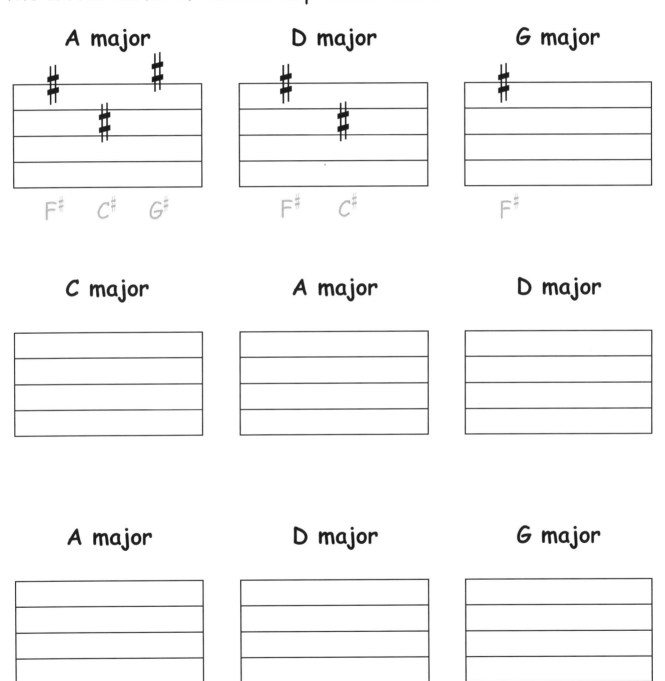

A major

F♯ C♯ G♯

D major

F♯ C♯

G major

F♯

C major

A major

D major

A major

D major

G major

Draw the correct number of sharps in each key signature and write the letter name of each sharp underneath.

G major

C major

D major

A major

G major

C major

C major

A major

G major

D major

C major

A major

Draw the correct number of sharps in each key signature and write the letter name of each sharp underneath.

A major	C major	D major

C major	G major	A major

G major	D major	A major

C major	D major	G major

Draw the correct number of sharps in each key signature and write the letter name of each sharp underneath.

G major

A major

D major

D major

C major

A major

A major

G major

C major

C major

A major

G major

DRAWING FLATS

When drawing flats, make sure the middle of the flat is on a space or line.

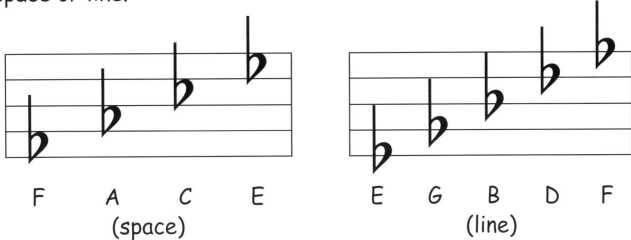

F   A   C   E   E   G   B   D   F

(space)   (line)

Write the name of the flat in the box below. Look carefully to see if the flat is on a space or line.

15

Write the name of the flat in the box below. Look carefully to
see if the flat is on a space or line.

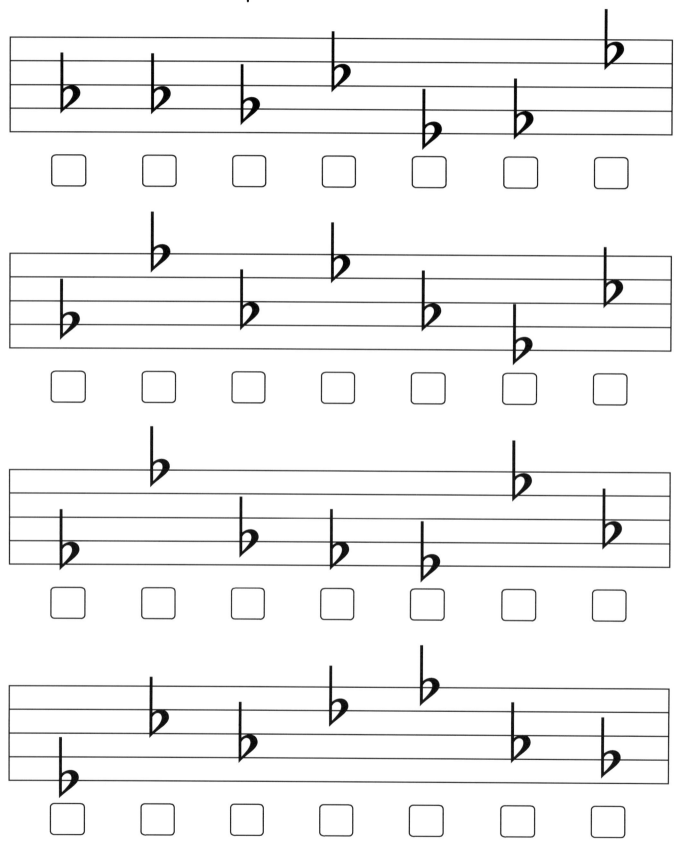

Use the flat name below to draw the flat on the space or line where it belongs.

| F | C | A | B | E | D | F |

| A | C | E | D | B | C | A |

| B | A | B | D | C | E | F |

| D | F | A | C | A | B | D |

Use the flat name below to draw the flat on the space or line where it belongs.

[staff]

B   A   E   D   F   B   C

[staff]

C   E   F   D   A   D   F

[staff]

F   A   C   E   F   D   B

[staff]

A   B   F   D   A   B   E

18

Draw flats on the music staff using the words below.

B   E   D

F   A   C   E

C   A   B

D   E   A   F

C   A   F   E

E   G   G

D   A   D

D   A   B

19

Fill in the boxes and find out what words appear using the flats below.

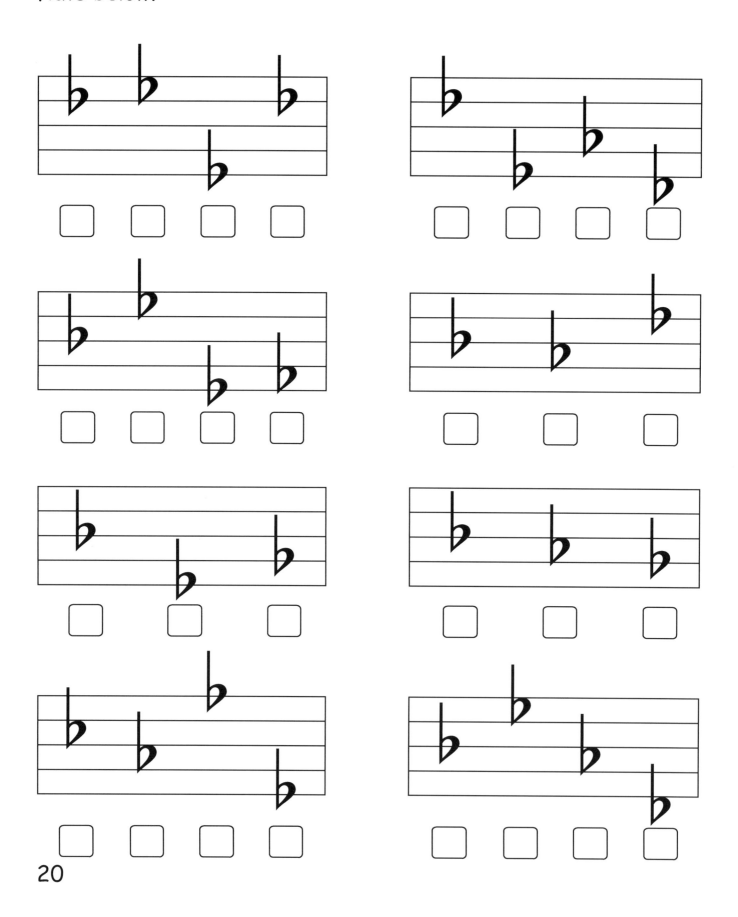

ORDER OF FLATS

Written music has seven flats which are always placed after the treble clef.

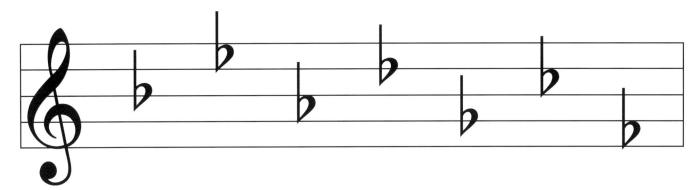

Each of these sharps are on a specific space or line and are always in this order.

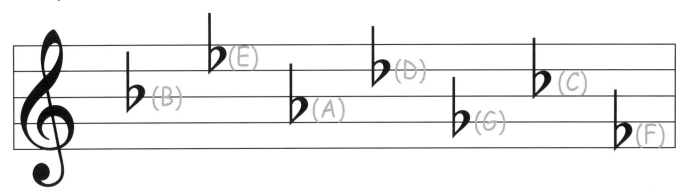

Here is an easy way to remember them. Use this saying:

Battle Ends And Down Goes Charles Father
1   2   3   4   5   6   7

This is the order of the sharps saying backwards!

What are the seven flats? List from left to right.

_____ _____ _____ _____ _____ _____ _____

Write the names of the seven flats in order using the
boxes below.
Here is an example.

Draw the seven flats in the correct order and write their names underneath.

LEARNING KEY SIGNATURES WITH FLATS

Key signatures are important because they let you know where to put your fingers on the violin. Key signatures are always written after the treble clef.

There are **4** important flat key signatures you should know.

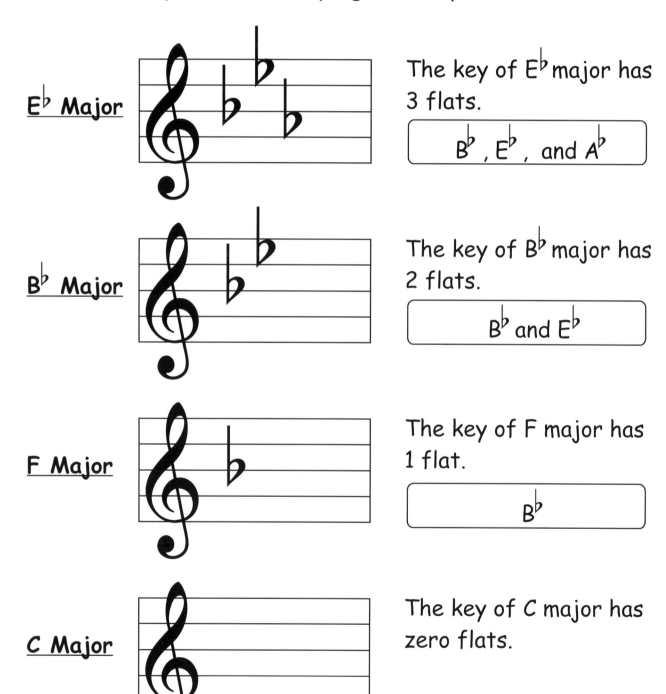

E♭ Major

The key of E♭ major has 3 flats.

B♭, E♭, and A♭

B♭ Major

The key of B♭ major has 2 flats.

B♭ and E♭

F Major

The key of F major has 1 flat.

B♭

C Major

The key of C major has zero flats.

DRAWING KEY SIGNATURES WITH FLATS

To draw key signatures with flats, you will need to remember the saying you learned earlier. For this exercise, draw the correct number of flats in each key signature and write the letter name of each flat underneath.

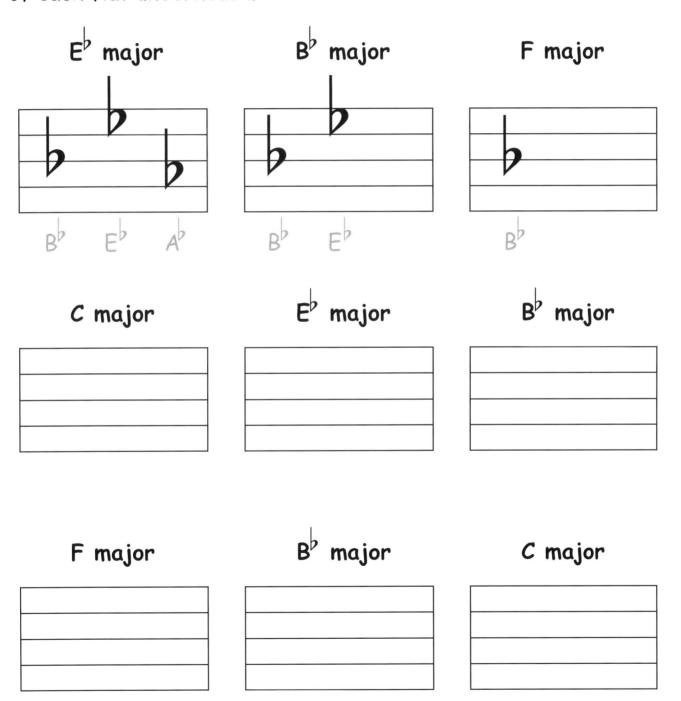

E♭ major

B♭ major

F major

B♭ E♭ A♭

B♭ E♭

B♭

C major

E♭ major

B♭ major

F major

B♭ major

C major

Draw the correct number of flats in each key signature and write the letter name of each flat underneath.

E♭ major B♭ major F major

B♭ major F major C major

C major B♭ major E♭ major

F major E♭ major B♭ major

Draw the correct number of flats in each key signature and write the letter name of each flat underneath.

E♭ major   C major   B♭ major

F major   C major   F major

B♭ major   C major   B♭ major

C major   B♭ major   F major

Draw the correct number of flats in each key signature and write the letter name of each flat underneath.

B♭ major

F major

E♭ major

E♭ major

F major

C major

C major

B♭ major

E♭ major

F major

E♭ major

B♭ major

TIME SIGNATURE REVIEW

Time signatures are important because they let you know how many beats are in each bar.

To write a time signature, start at the beginning of the music. The time signature is always placed after any sharps or flats in the music.

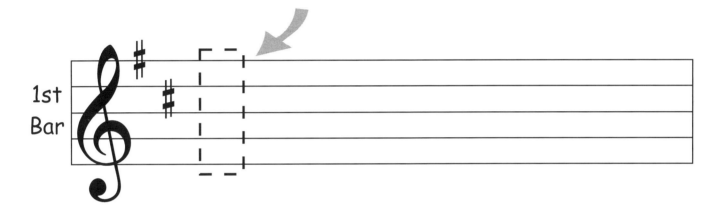

1st Bar

The time signature of the song looks like this. It will have a number on top and a number on the bottom.

The top number tells you how many beats there are in each bar.

4
4

The bottom number tells you the kind of note that each bar combination will have.

Example #1

This means that the combination of beats must be equal to quarter notes (1 beat each). → ← This means that there are 4 beats in each bar.

4 beats using 4 quarter notes

Note: $\frac{4}{4}$ time is called **quadruple time** or **common time** (C).

- -

Example #2

This means the combinations of notes must be equal to the quarter notes. →  ← This means that there are 3 beats in each bar.

Note: $\frac{3}{4}$ time is called **triple time**.

- -

Example #3

This means the combination of notes must be equal to quarter notes. →  ← This means that there are 2 beats in each bar.

DRAWING TIME SIGNATURES

Now it's your turn! Draw notes and rests in each bar.
You can choose any combination of notes and rests as long
as they equal the top number in the time signature.
Be sure to use different combinations of notes & rests.

Example

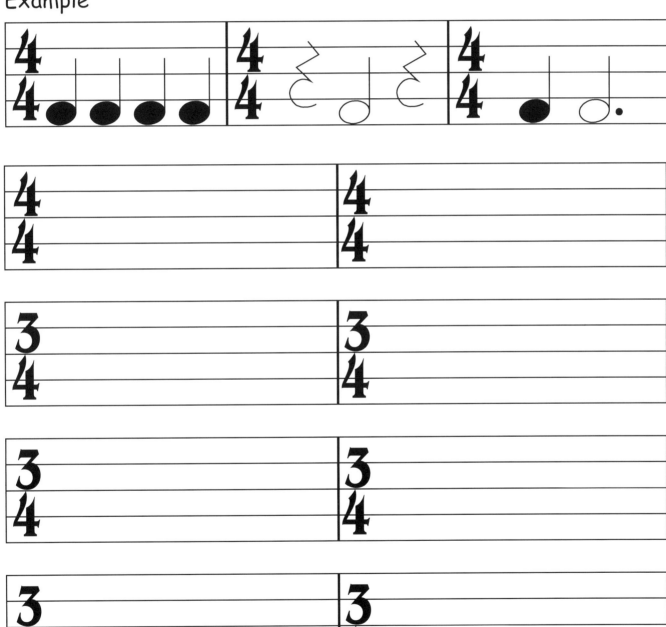

Make up your own combinations of notes and rests to fill each time signature.

$\begin{array}{c} 2 \\ \overline{4} \end{array}$

$\begin{array}{c} 2 \\ \overline{4} \end{array}$

$\begin{array}{c} 2 \\ \overline{4} \end{array}$

$\begin{array}{c} 2 \\ \overline{4} \end{array}$

$\begin{array}{c} 2 \\ \overline{4} \end{array}$

$\begin{array}{c} 2 \\ \overline{4} \end{array}$

$\begin{array}{c} 3 \\ \overline{4} \end{array}$

$\begin{array}{c} 4 \\ \overline{4} \end{array}$

$\begin{array}{c} 2 \\ \overline{4} \end{array}$

$\begin{array}{c} 4 \\ \overline{4} \end{array}$

$\begin{array}{c} 3 \\ \overline{4} \end{array}$

$\begin{array}{c} 2 \\ \overline{4} \end{array}$

The following bars don't have the correct number of beats to complete the time signature. Complete each bar by adding a note or rest to make the time signature correct.

Example

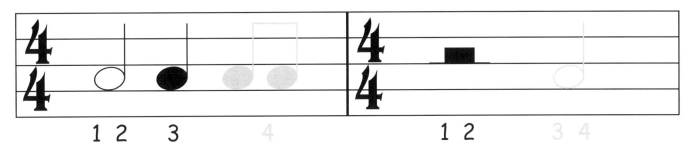

1 2   3   4   1 2   3 4

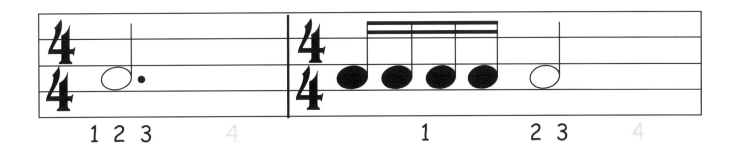

1 2 3   4   1   2 3   4

1 2   3   4   1   2 3   4

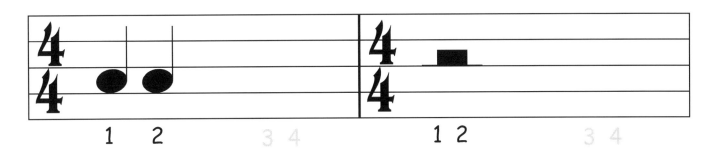

1   2   3 4   1 2   3 4

The following bars don't have the correct number of beats to complete the time signature. Complete each bar by adding a note or rest to make the time signature correct.

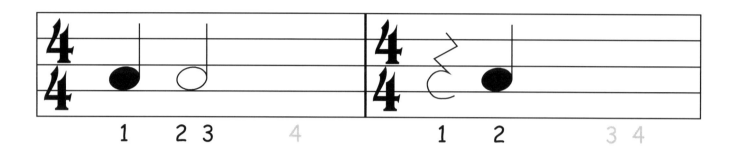

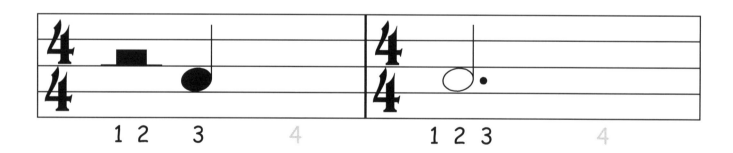

LEARNING TO WRITE MUSIC

Follow these steps. Write your music using the music staves beside each example.

① Draw a treble clef

② Add a key signature

③ Add a time signature

④ Add notes and a bar line

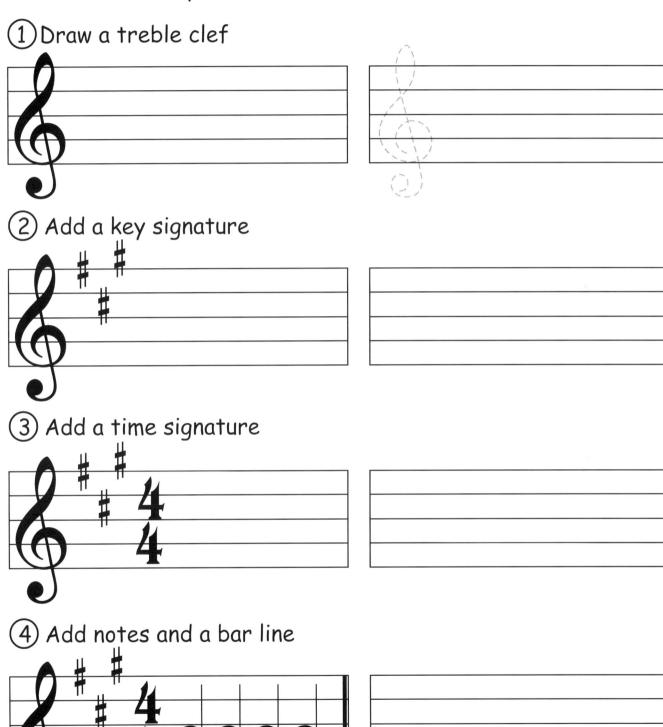

For these examples, use only the open A to draw your notes on.

① Draw a treble clef, A major key signature, $\frac{4}{4}$ time signature, any combination of notes or rests, and a bar line.

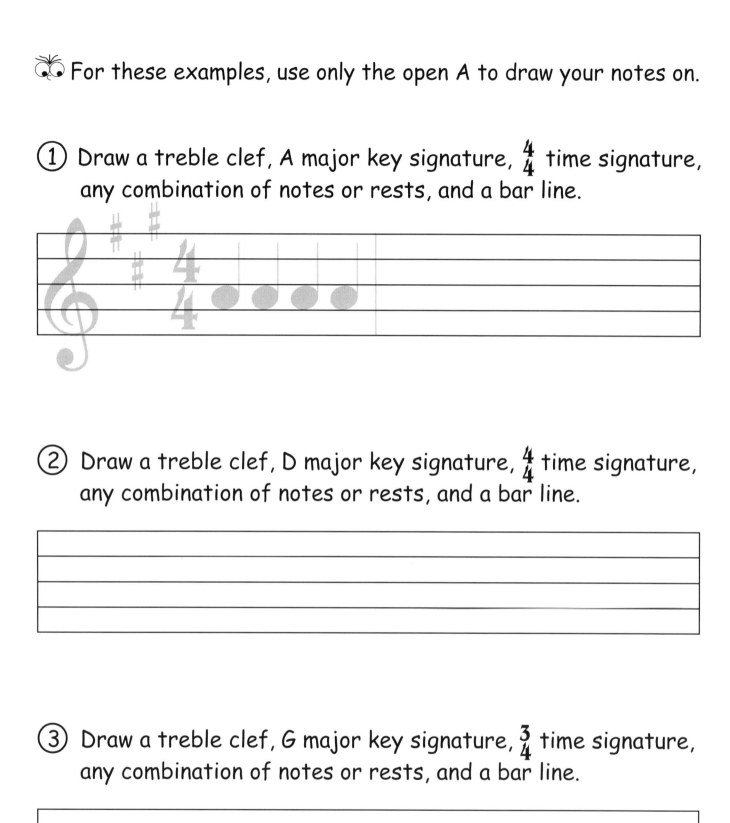

② Draw a treble clef, D major key signature, $\frac{4}{4}$ time signature, any combination of notes or rests, and a bar line.

③ Draw a treble clef, G major key signature, $\frac{3}{4}$ time signature, any combination of notes or rests, and a bar line.

🐞 For these examples, use only the open A to draw your notes on.

④ Draw a treble clef, C major key signature, $\frac{4}{4}$ time signature, any combination of notes or rests, and a bar line.

⑤ Draw a treble clef, A♭ major key signature, $\frac{4}{4}$ time signature, any combination of notes or rests, and a bar line.

⑥ Draw a treble clef, B♭ major key signature, $\frac{2}{4}$ time signature, any combination of notes or rests, and a bar line.

🐞 For these examples, use only the open A to draw your notes on.

⑦ Draw a treble clef, F major key signature, $\frac{3}{4}$ time signature, any combination of notes or rests, and a bar line.

⑧ Draw a treble clef, A major key signature, $\frac{4}{4}$ time signature, any combination of notes or rests, and a bar line.

⑨ Draw a treble clef, A♭ major key signature, $\frac{2}{4}$ time signature, any combination of notes or rests, and a bar line.

For these examples, use only the open A to draw your notes on.

(10) Draw a treble clef, D major key signature, $\frac{4}{4}$ time signature, any combination of notes or rests, and a bar line.

(11) Draw a treble clef, B♭ major key signature, $\frac{3}{4}$ time signature, any combination of notes or rests, and a bar line.

(12) Draw a treble clef, G major key signature, $\frac{2}{4}$ time signature, any combination of notes or rests, and a bar line.

MAKE UP YOUR OWN MUSIC

Choose from these key signatures:

A major   F♯ C♯ G♯   E♭ major   B♭ E♭ A♭

D major   F♯ C♯   B♭ major   B♭ E♭

G major   F♯   F major   B♭

C major

Choose from these time signatures:

$\frac{2}{4}$ $\frac{3}{4}$ $\frac{4}{4}$

For this exercise, fill in 2 bars of music using different combinations of notes and rests. Only use the open A.

Example 1.

The key signature will be <u>D major</u>. The time signature will be ___$\frac{3}{4}$___.

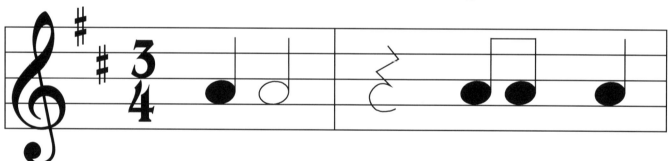

Exercise 1.

The key signature will be _____. The time signature will be _____.

Exercise 2.

The key signature will be _____.The time signature will be ____.

Exercise 3.

The key signature will be _____.The time signature will be ____.

Exercise 4.

The key signature will be _____.The time signature will be ____.

Exercise 5.

The key signature will be _____. The time signature will be _____.

```
┌─────────────────────────────────────────────────────────────┐
│                                                               │
│                                                               │
│                                                               │
│                                                               │
└─────────────────────────────────────────────────────────────┘
```

Exercise 6.

The key signature will be _____. The time signature will be _____.

```
┌─────────────────────────────────────────────────────────────┐
│                                                               │
│                                                               │
│                                                               │
│                                                               │
└─────────────────────────────────────────────────────────────┘
```

Exercise 7.

The key signature will be _____. The time signature will be _____.

```
┌─────────────────────────────────────────────────────────────┐
│                                                               │
│                                                               │
│                                                               │
│                                                               │
└─────────────────────────────────────────────────────────────┘
```

Exercise 8.

The key signature will be _____. The time signature will be _____.

```
_____
_____
_____
_____
```

Exercise 9.

The key signature will be _____. The time signature will be _____.

```
_____
_____
_____
_____
```

Exercise 10.

The key signature will be _____. The time signature will be _____.

```
_____
_____
_____
_____
```

WRITING MUSIC

Before you write your own music, it is important to know that
the stem on the side of the note changes from up to down on
space 3. You also need to know that the stem on the B can go up
or down depending on the note before.

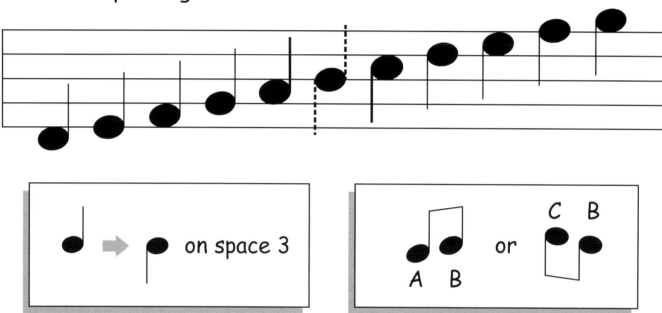

For this exercise, fill in 2 bars of music using different
combinations of notes and rests. You can use all the notes
you know.

Example 1.

The key signature will be _G major_ . The time signature will be _4/4_ .

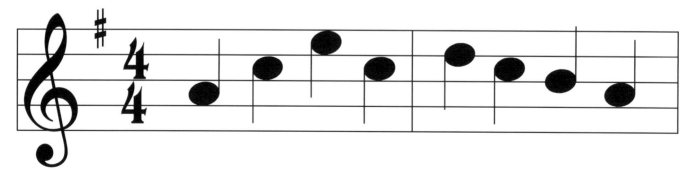

Example 2.

The key signature will be ___F major___. The time signature will be $\frac{3}{4}$.

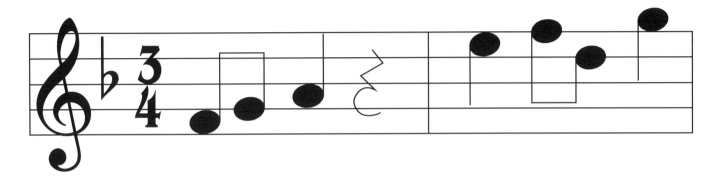

Exercise 1.

The key signature will be _____. The time signature will be ___.

Exercise 2.

The key signature will be _____. The time signature will be ___.

Exercise 3.

The key signature will be _____ . The time signature will be ___ .

```
┌─────────────────────────────────────────────────┐
│                                                   │
├───────────────────────────────────────────────────┤
├───────────────────────────────────────────────────┤
├───────────────────────────────────────────────────┤
└───────────────────────────────────────────────────┘
```

Exercise 4.

The key signature will be _____ . The time signature will be ___ .

```
┌─────────────────────────────────────────────────┐
│                                                   │
├───────────────────────────────────────────────────┤
├───────────────────────────────────────────────────┤
├───────────────────────────────────────────────────┤
└───────────────────────────────────────────────────┘
```

Exercise 5.

The key signature will be _____ . The time signature will be ___ .

```
┌─────────────────────────────────────────────────┐
│                                                   │
├───────────────────────────────────────────────────┤
├───────────────────────────────────────────────────┤
├───────────────────────────────────────────────────┤
└───────────────────────────────────────────────────┘
```

Exercise 6.

The key signature will be _____ . The time signature will be ___ .

Exercice 7.

The key signature will be _____ . The time signature will be ___ .

Exercice 8.

The key signature will be _____ . The time signature will be ___ .

Exercise 9.

The key signature will be _____. The time signature will be ___.

Exercise 10.

The key signature will be _____. The time signature will be ___.

Exercise 11.

The key signature will be _____. The time signature will be ___.

SHARPS, NATURALS, AND FLATS

Sharps, naturals, and flats are used in music to change the sound of the notes.

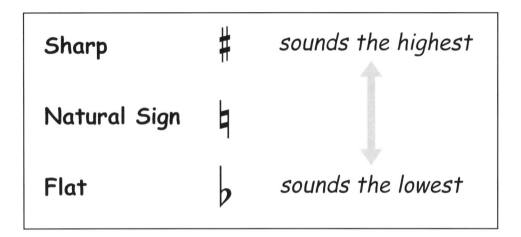

Definitions

Sharp - raises the note a semitone or a half step.
Natural Sign - cancels out a sharp or flat.
Flat - lowers the note a semitone or a half step.

Here is a general rule:

♭ → ♮ → ♯   ♯ → ♮ → ♭

(note becomes higher)   (note becomes lower)

Do these notes go higher or lower? Fill in the blanks.

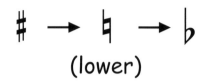

♭ → ♮ → ♯
(higher)

♯ → ♮ → ♭
(lower)

1. ♯ → ♮   (lower) _____

2. ♭ → ♮   _____

3. ♯ → ♮   _____

4. ♮ → ♭   _____

5. ♯ → ♮   _____

6. ♭ → ♮   _____

7. ♯ → ♮   _____

8. ♮ → ♭   _____

9. ♯ → ♮   _____

10. ♭ → ♮   _____

11. ♮ → ♭   _____

12. ♯ → ♮   _____

50

NOTES ON THE VIOLIN

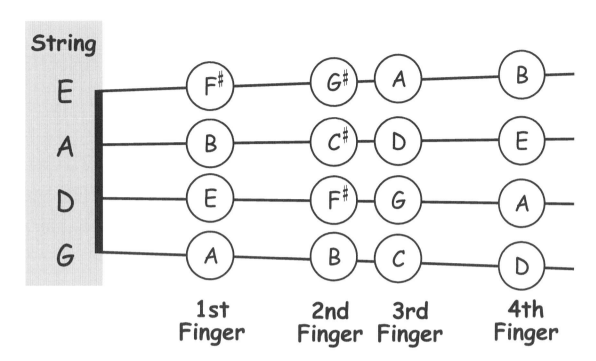

String	1st Finger	2nd Finger	3rd Finger	4th Finger

 Remember if the note is just a letter such as E, it means E♮.

Answer the following questions using the circled notes only.

Using your fingers:

How many (A) notes can you play? _____3_____

How many (B) notes can you play? _____

How many (C) notes can you play? _____

How many (D) notes can you play? _____

How many (E) notes can you play? _____

How many (F) notes can you play? _____

How many (G) notes can you play? _____

Fill in the appropriate note names on the violin diagram.

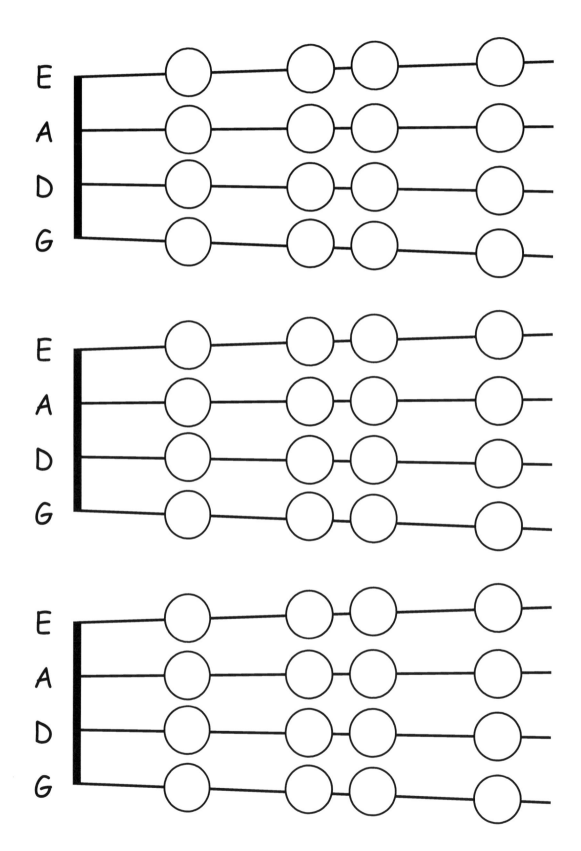

BEGINNER ENHARMONICS

An <u>enharmonic</u> is when the same note has 2 different names.

All the boxes are enharmonics.

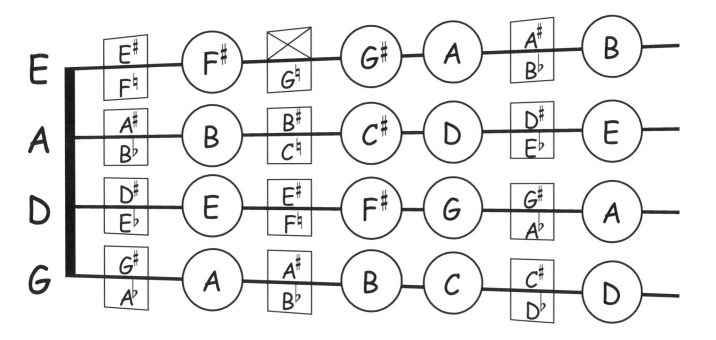

Whether the enharmonic is a sharp, natural or flat depends on the direction that your fingers are coming from.

1ST FINGER ENHARMONICS

All these enharmonics can be played with the 1st finger.

Remember: whether it's a sharp, natural or flat depends on the direction that your fingers are coming from.

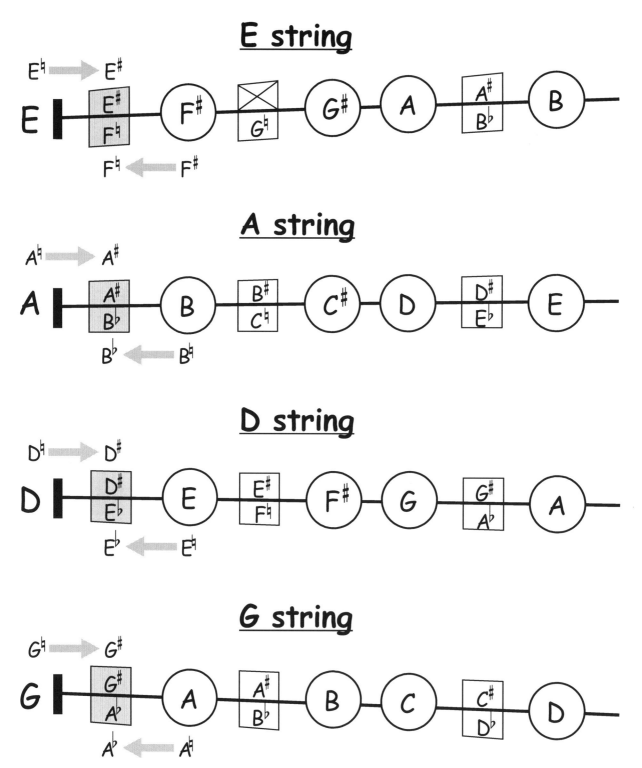

54

What are the 4 enharmonics pairs you can play with
your 1st finger?

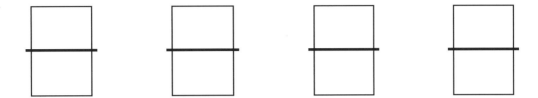

Which note is higher? Circle the higher note. If the notes are
the same, circle both. Use the diagram to help you.

E string	A string	D string	G string
E or F♮	A or A♯	D or E	G or G♯
F♯ or E♯	A♯ or B	E or D♯	G♯ or A
E or F♯	B♭ or A	E or E♭	A or A♭
F♮ or E♯	B♮ or A♯	E♭ or D	A♭ or G
E or F♯	B♭ or A♯	D or D♯	G or G♯

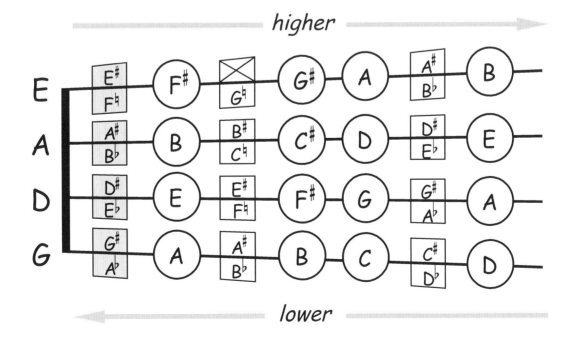

Which note is lower? Circle the lower note. If the notes are the same, circle both. Use the diagram to help you.

E string	A string	D string	G string
E or F♮	A or A♯	D or E	G or G♯
F♯ or E♯	A♯ or B	E or D♯	G♯ or A
E or F♯	B♭ or A	E or E♭	A or A♭
F♮ or E♯	B♮ or A♯	E♭ or D	A♭ or G
E or F♯	B♭ or A♯	D or D♯	G or G♯

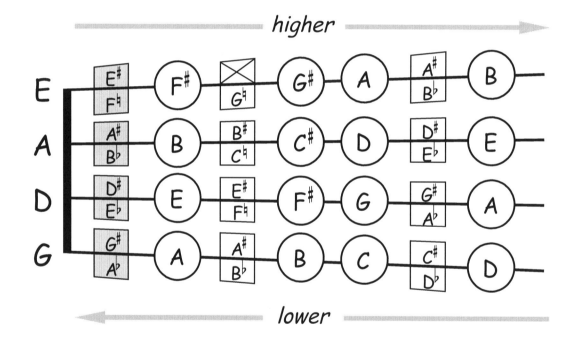

Challenging Question: What is an enharmonic?

_____

_____

_____

_____

1ST & 2ND FINGER ENHARMONICS

You can play all these enharmonics with either your 1st or 2nd finger.

If you go in ➡ direction, use 1st finger.
If you go in ⬅ direction, use 2nd finger.

E string

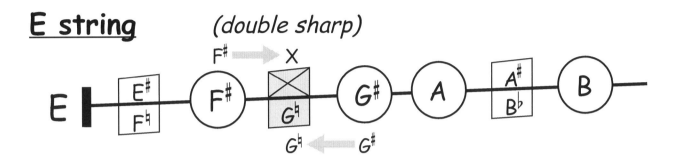

A string

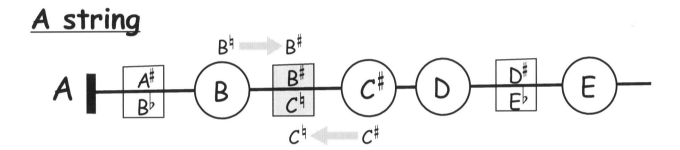

D string

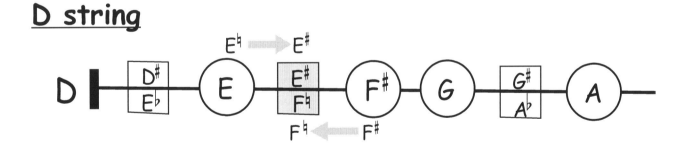

G string

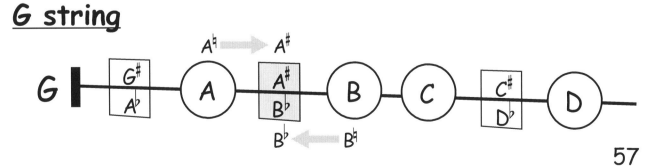

What are the 4 enharmonics pairs you can play with
your 1st and 2nd finger?

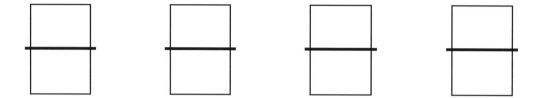

Which note is higher? Circle the higher note. If the notes are
the same, circle both. Use the diagram to help you.

E string	A string	D string	G string
F♯ or G♮	B or C♯	E or E♯	A or A♯
F♯ or G♯	B♯ or B	F♮ or F♯	A♯ or B
G♯ or G♮	C♮ or C♯	F♮ or E	B♭ or A
F♯ or G♯	B or C♮	F♯ or F♮	A♯ or B♭
G♮ or F♯	C♮ or C♯	E or E♯	B or B♭

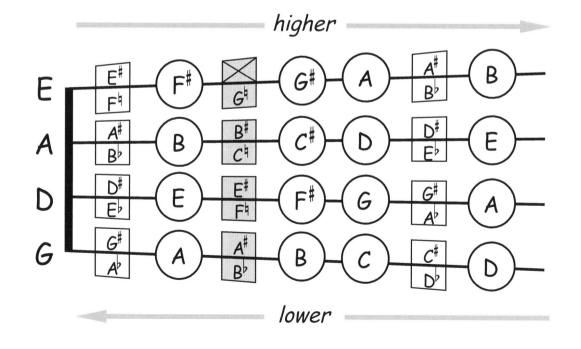

Which note is lower? Circle the lower note. If the notes are the same, circle both. Use the diagram to help you.

E string	**A string**	**D string**	**G string**
F♯ or G♮	B or C♯	E or E♯	A or A♯
F♯ or G♯	B♯ or B	F♮ or F♯	A♯ or B
G♯ or G♮	C♮ or C♯	F♮ or E	B♭ or A
F♯ or G♯	B or C♮	F♯ or F♮	A♯ or B♭
G♮ or F♯	C♮ or C♯	E or E♯	B or B♭

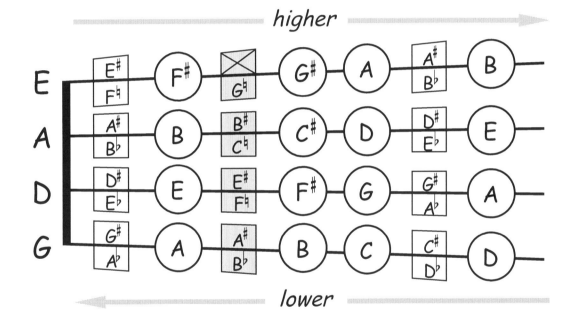

Challenging Question:
What is different about the enharmonic pair on the E string?

_____

_____

_____

_____

3RD & 4TH FINGER ENHARMONICS

You can play all these enharmonics with either your 3rd or 4th finger.

If you go in ➡ direction, use 3rd finger.
If you go in ⬅ direction, use 4th finger.

E string

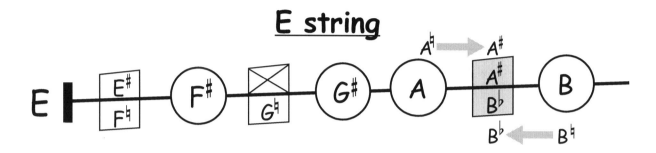

A string

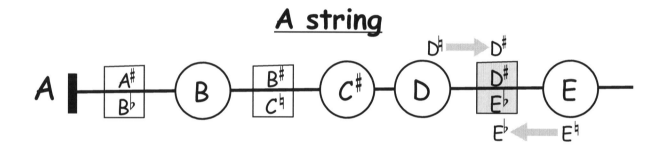

D string

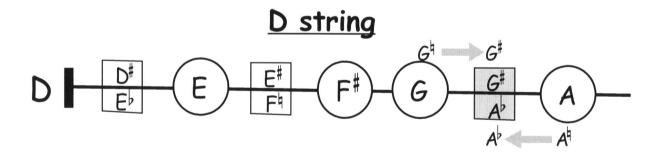

G string

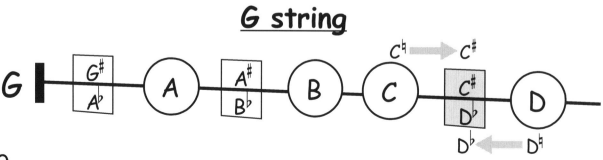

What are the 4 enharmonics pairs you can play with
your 3rd and 4th finger?

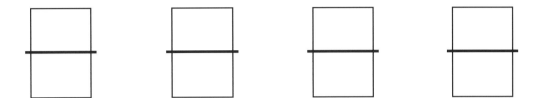

Which note is higher? Circle the higher note. If the notes are
the same, circle both. Use the diagram to help you.

E string	A string	D string	G string
A or B♭	E or D♯	A♭ or G♯	C or D♭
A♯ or B	E♭ or D	G♮ or A♭	D or D♭
B♭ or A♯	E♭ or E	A or G	C♯ or C
B♭ or A	D or D♯	G or A♭	D or D♭
B or A♯	D♯ or E♭	G♯ or G	C♯ or D

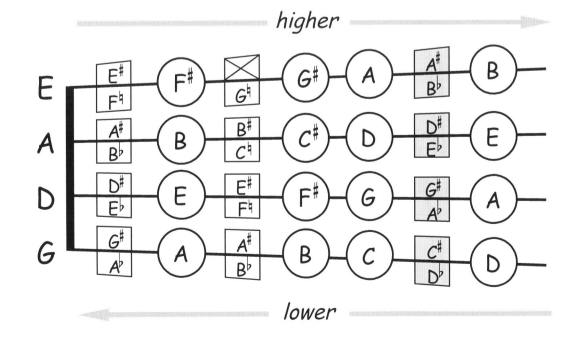

Which note is lower? Circle the lower note. If the notes are the same, circle both. Use the diagram to help you.

E string	A string	D string	G string
A or B♭	E or D♯	A♭ or G♯	C or D♭
A♯ or B	E♭ or D	G♮ or A♭	D or D♭
B♭ or A♯	E♭ or E	A or G	C♯ or C
B♭ or A	D or D♯	G or A♭	D or D♭
B or A♯	D♯ or E♭	G♯ or G	C♯ or D

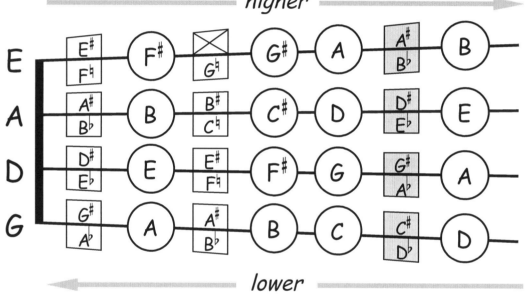

Challenging Question:
List all the enharmonic pairs you have learned. (Hint - there are 12 pairs)

E string

A string

D string

G string

ENHARMONICS REVIEW

Fill in the following charts. Add the correct notes.

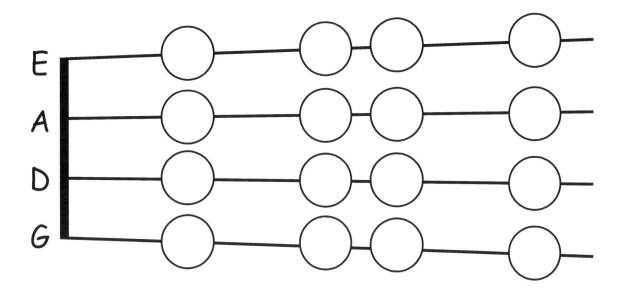

Add the correct notes and enharmonic pairs.

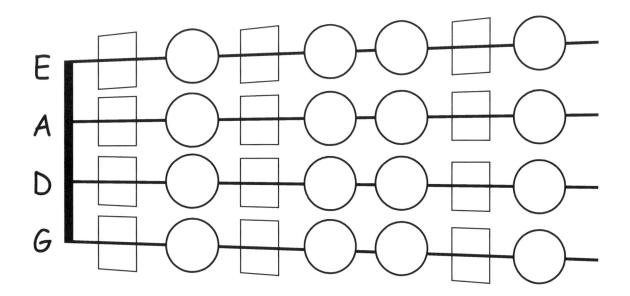

SEMITONES

A semitone (ST) is also called a half step and is a small move for the finger on the violin.

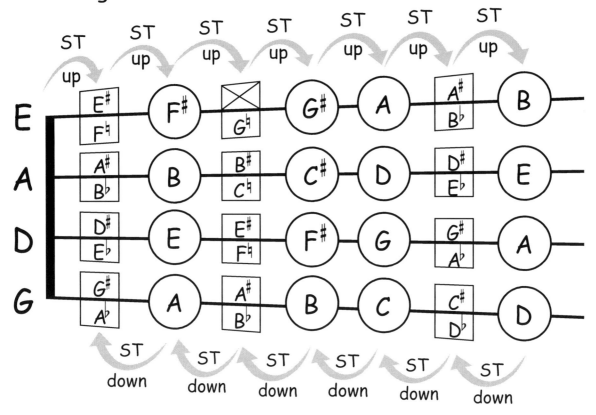

What are 12 examples of semitones? Remember, semitones can go up or down.

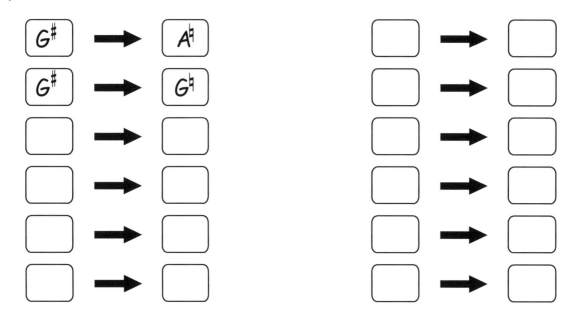

There are 2 kinds of semitones in violin - chromatic semitones and diatonic semitones.

Chromatic Semitones

A chromatic semitone is when a note moves a half step to a note with the same letter name. This move usually done with the same finger and is called a finger slide.

ie.) $C^\sharp \longrightarrow C^\natural$

$E^\flat \longrightarrow E^\natural$

$F^\sharp \longrightarrow F^\natural$

Here are the <u>E string</u> chromatic semitones on the violin.

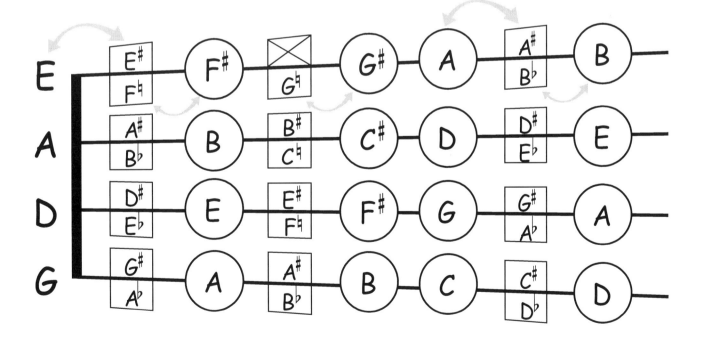

65

Now it's your turn. Fill in the rest of the arrows on the diagram to show every chromatic semitone on the violin.
Start at the open string.

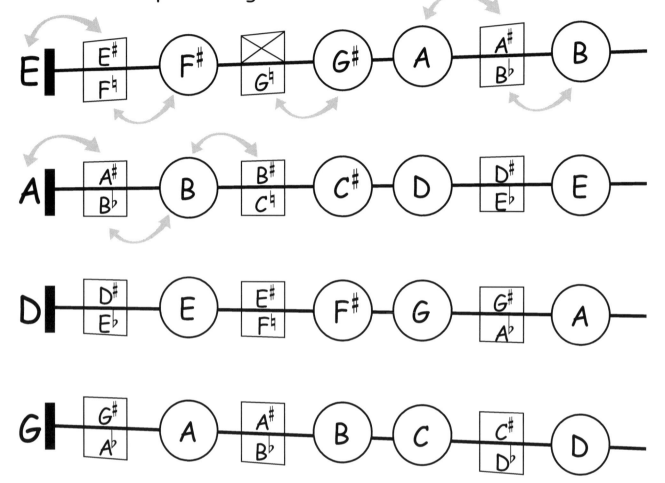

Name 10 chromatic semitones. You can choose any letter and go up or down. Remember - the notes have to be the same letter.

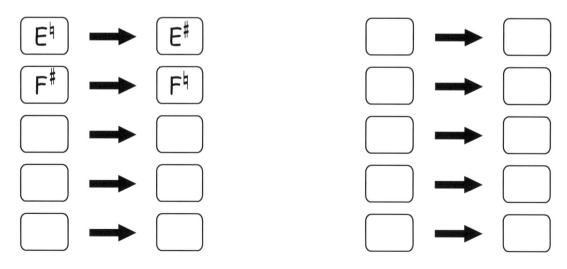

Diatonic Semitones

A Diatonic semitone is when a note moves a half step to a note with a different name. This move is usually done with a different finger.

ie.)   F♯ ⟶ G♮

        A♭ ⟶ G♮

        B♮ ⟶ C♮

Here are the <u>E string</u> diatonic semitones on the violin.

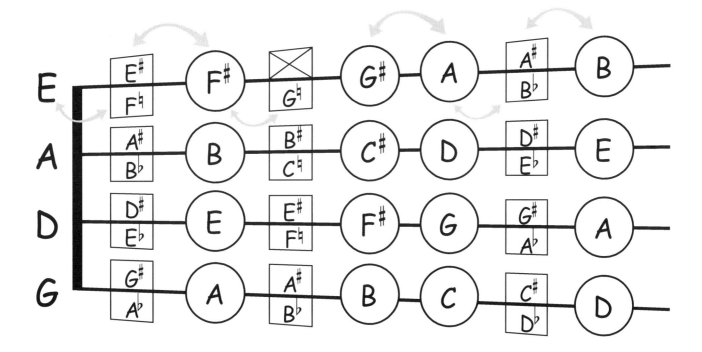

Now it's your turn. Fill in the rest of the arrows on the diagram to show every diatonic semitone on the violin.
Start at the open string.

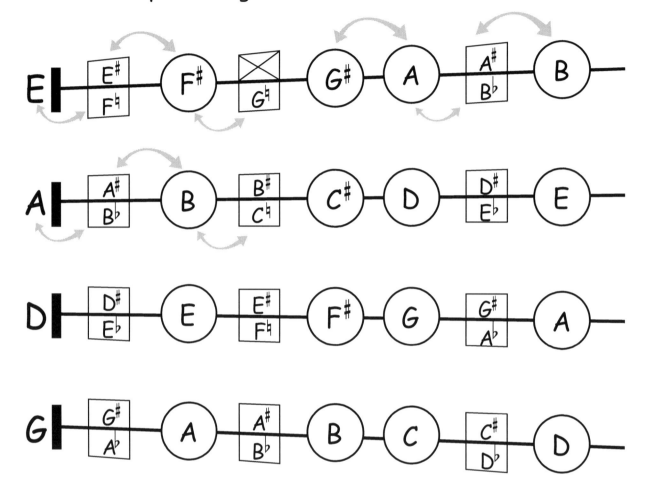

Name 10 diatonic semitones. You can choose any letter and go up or down. Remember - the notes have to be a different letter.

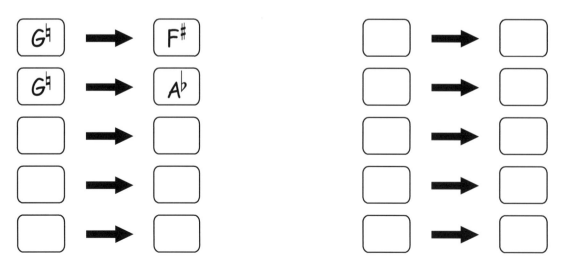

SEMITONES REVIEW

Chromatic Semitones

 Remember - you only move one half step up or down to a note with the same letter.

What is a chromatic semitone of:

F♯ ➡ [F♮]   D♭ ➡ [ ]

G♮ ➡ [ ]   E♮ ➡ [ ]

A♭ ➡ [ ]   F♮ ➡ [ ]

B♮ ➡ [ ]   G♯ ➡ [ ]

C♯ ➡ [ ]   A♮ ➡ [ ]

Diatonic Semitones

 Remember - you only move one half step up or down to a note with a different letter.

What is a diatonic semitone of:

F♯ ➡ [G♭ or E♯]   D♭ ➡ [ ]

G♮ ➡ [ ]   E♮ ➡ [ ]

A♭ ➡ [ ]   F♮ ➡ [ ]

B♮ ➡ [ ]   G♯ ➡ [ ]

C♯ ➡ [ ]   A♮ ➡ [ ]

WHOLETONES

A wholetone (WT) is a 2 semitone move up or down on the violin.

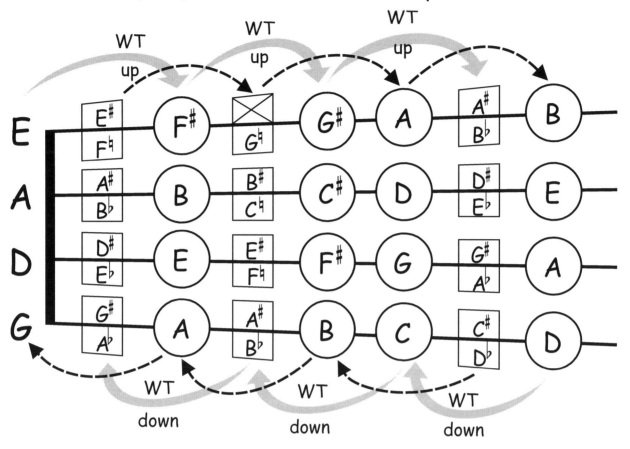

What are 12 examples of wholetones? Remember wholetones can move up or down.

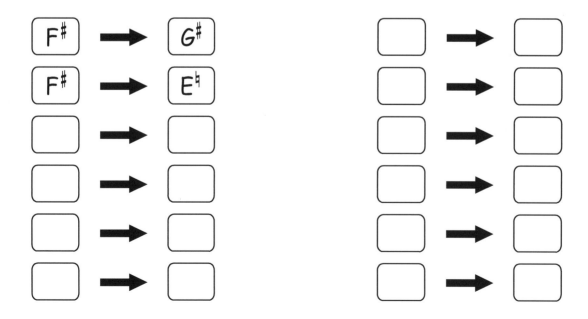

Fill in the rest of the arrows on the diagram to show every wholetone on the violin. Start with each open string.

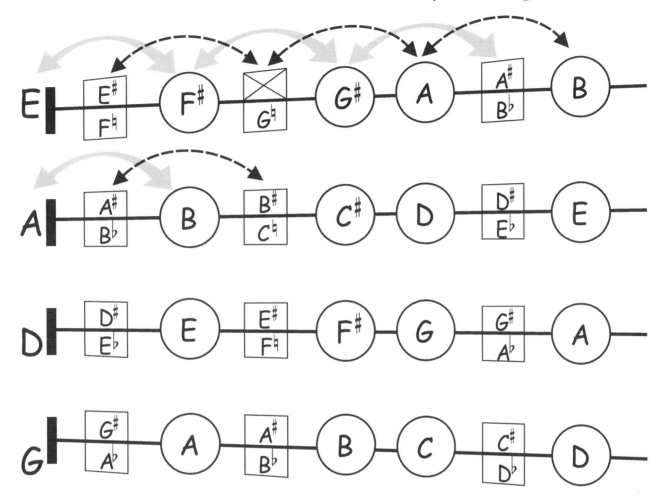

Wholetones Review

 Remember - move 2 half steps up or down.

What is a wholetone of:

F♯ ⟹ G♯ or E♮ or A♭

G♮ ⟹ F♮ or A♮ or E♯

A♭ ⟹ [   ]

B♮ ⟹ [   ]

C♯ ⟹ [   ]

D♭ ⟹ [   ]

E♮ ⟹ [   ]

F♮ ⟹ [   ]

G♯ ⟹ [   ]

A♮ ⟹ [   ]

SEMITONE AND WHOLETONES REVIEW

Use this diagram for help.

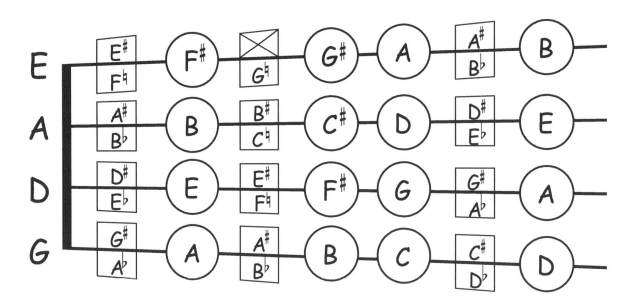

Fill in the blanks.

chromatic semitones   diatonic semitones   wholetones

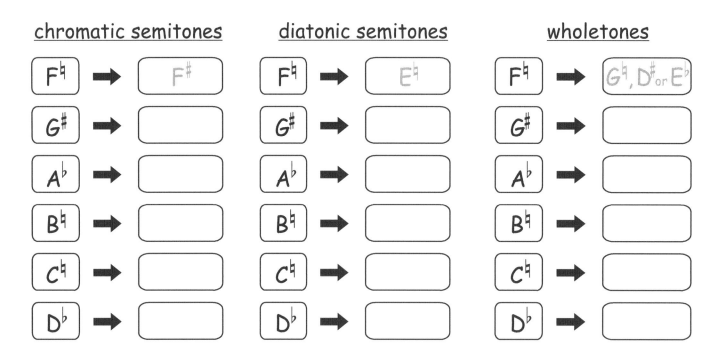

MAJOR SCALES

A scale is a pattern of 8 notes that go up in pitch and down in pitch.

Think of a scale like a ladder.

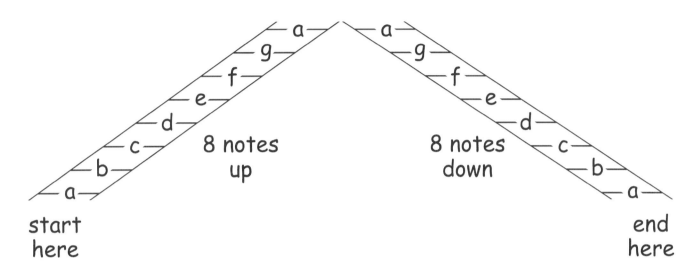

8 notes up

8 notes down

start here

end here

OCTAVE

This pattern of eight notes is also called an octave.

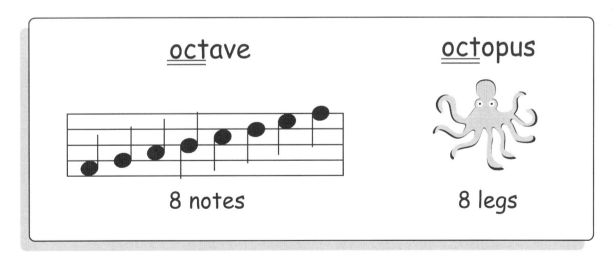

octave

octopus

8 notes

8 legs

Therefore, a scale is an octave going up
and an octave going down.

"A MAJOR" SCALE (2 PARTS)

The first scale we'll cover is the A MAJOR SCALE

The key of A major
has 3 sharps.

| F# | C# | G# |

To write the A major scale, begin with the first letter of the
key signature and count up 8 notes.

 Remember after the G, you start again with the A.

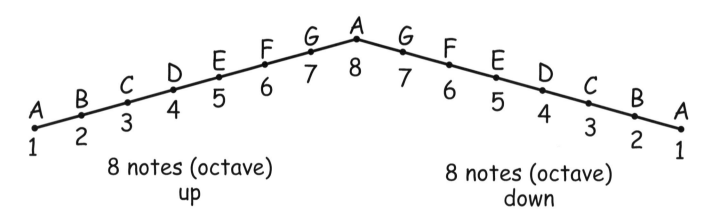

8 notes (octave)
up

8 notes (octave)
down

Now add sharps to every F, C, and G.

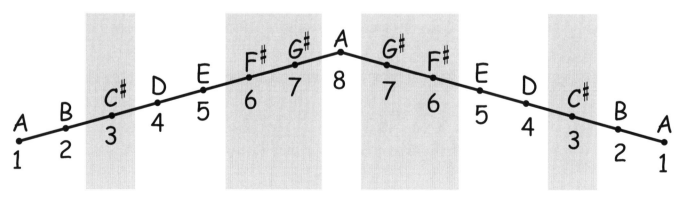

When you write a scale on the music staff, you use the same technique you learned on the previous page.

Start on open A and draw 8 notes up and 8 notes down.

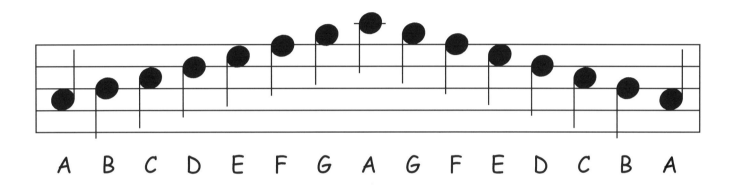

Now add sharps to every F, C, and G. Remember, the sharps are always put before the music note - not after.

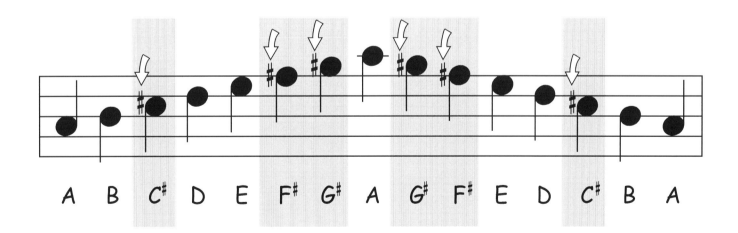

Now it's your turn!

Write the notes in the A major scale and add sharps to every F, C and G.

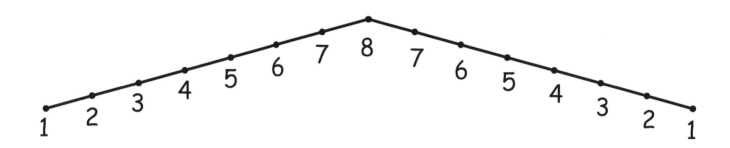

Write the A major scale using quarter notes. Start on open A and label the sharps. Write the note names underneath.

PLAYING THE "A MAJOR" SCALE ON THE VIOLIN

Using the A major scale below, notice where the notes in the scale are on the violin.

Notice that there are no enharmonic notes in this scale!

The numbers on top of the notes are the fingers you could use to play the scale.

Look carefully to see where the notes in the scale begin and end on the violin.

Use the music staff below to write the A major scale.

Using the scale above, fill in the appropriate note names on the violin diagram.

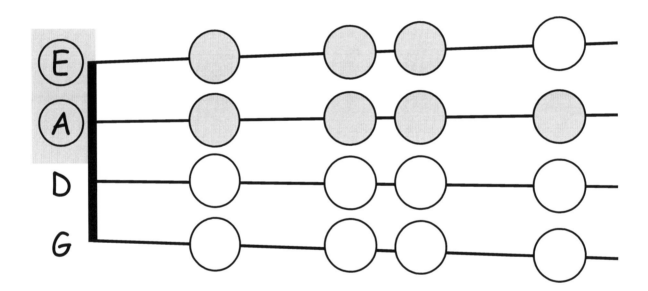

Challenging Question:
Were there any enharmonic notes in the A major scale above?

Yes or No

If so, what were they? _____

Fill in the appropriate note names on the violin diagram.

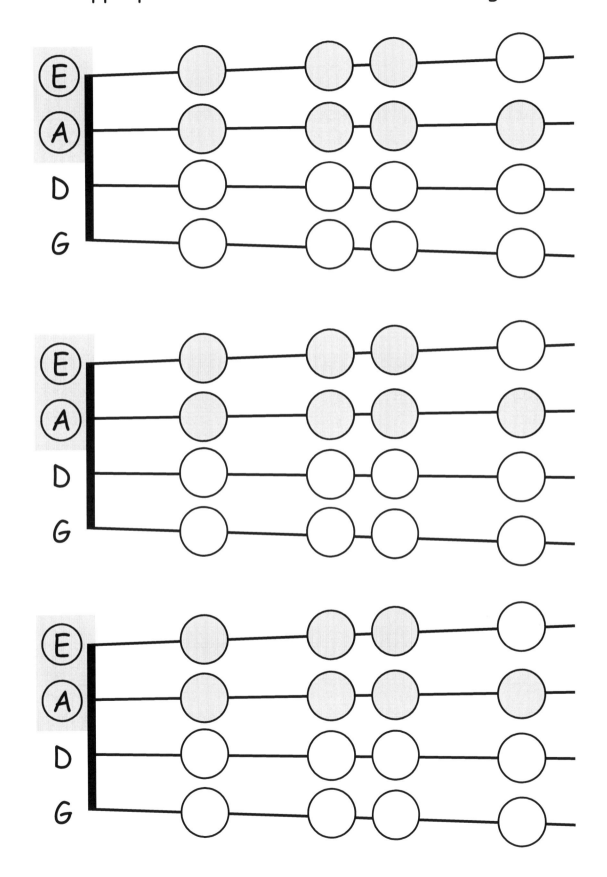

When you write a scale on the music staff, you use the same technique you learned on the previous page.

Start on low A and draw 8 notes up and 8 notes down.

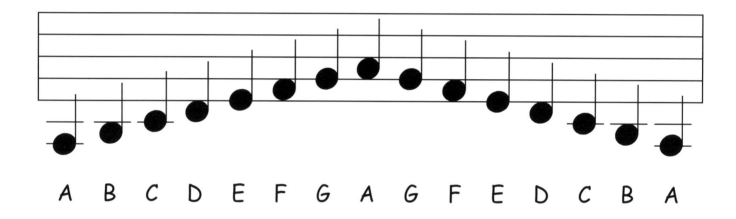

A B C D E F G A G F E D C B A

Now add sharps to every F, C, and G. Remember, the sharps are always put before the music note - not after.

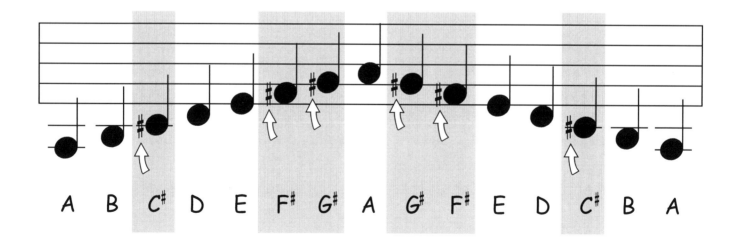

A B C# D E F# G# A G# F# E D C# B A

80

Now it's your turn!

Write the notes in the A major scale and add sharps to every
F, C and G.

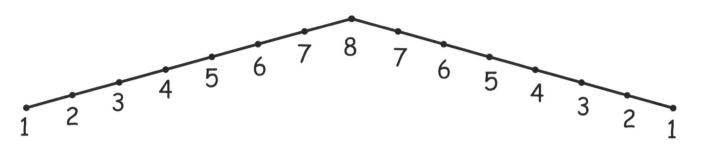

Write the A major scale using quarter notes. Start on low A and
label the sharps. Write the note names underneath.

PLAYING THE "A MAJOR" SCALE ON THE VIOLIN

Using the A major scale below, notice where the notes in the scale are on the violin. Notice that there are two enharmonic notes in this scale - C♯ and G♯.

The numbers on top of the notes are the fingers you could use to play the scale.

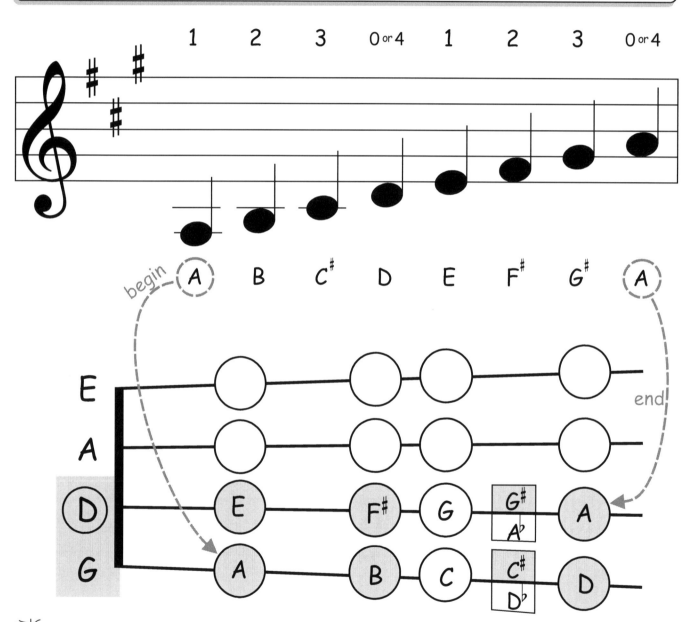

👀 Look carefully to see where the notes in the scale begin and end on the violin.

Use the music staff below to write the A major scale.

Using the scale above, fill in the appropriate note names on the violin diagram.

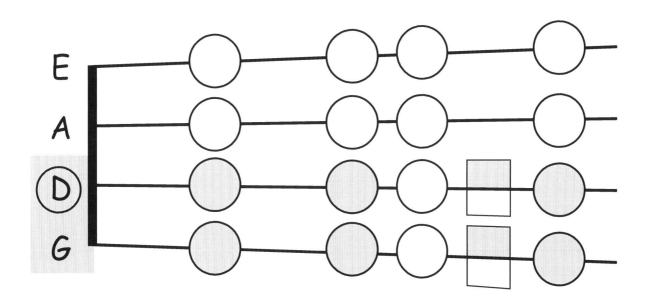

Challenging Question:
Were there any enharmonic notes in the A major scale above?

Yes or No

If so, what were they? _____

Fill in the appropriate note names on the violin diagram.

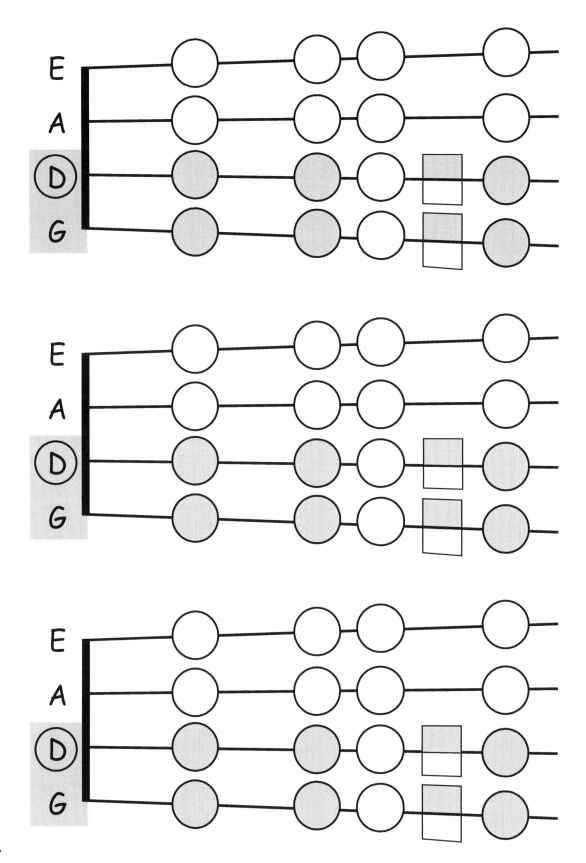

"D MAJOR" SCALE

The second scale we'll cover is the **D MAJOR SCALE**

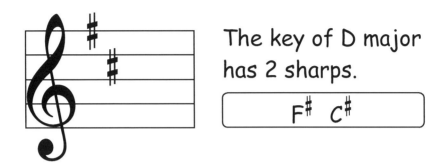

The key of D major has 2 sharps.

F# C#

To write the D major scale, begin with the first letter of the key signature and count up 8 notes.

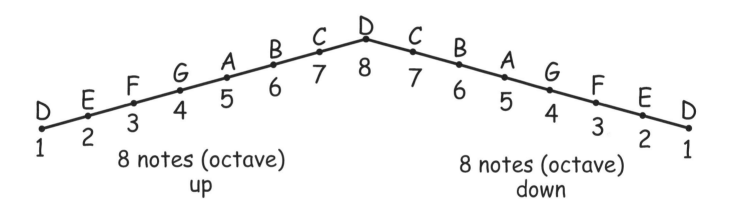

8 notes (octave) up

8 notes (octave) down

Now add sharps to every F and C.

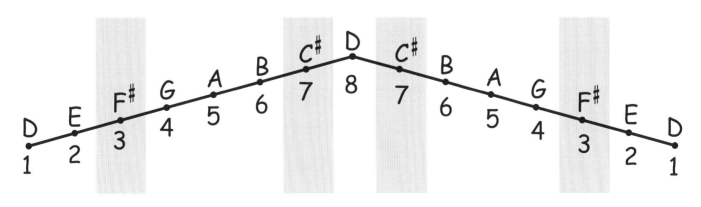

When you write a scale on the music staff, you use the same technique you learned on the previous page.

Start on open D and draw 8 notes up and 8 notes down.

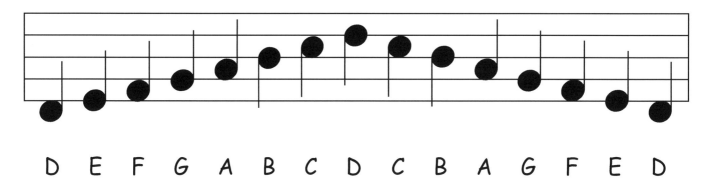

D E F G A B C D C B A G F E D

Now add sharps to every F and C. Remember, the sharps are always put before the music note - not after.

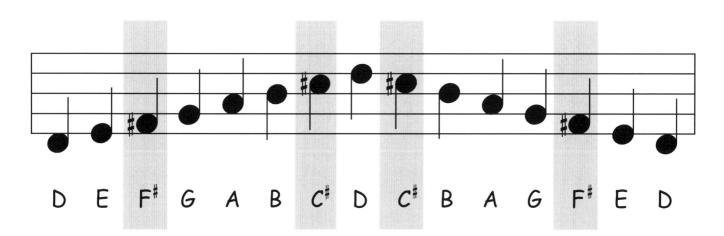

D E F# G A B C# D C# B A G F# E D

 Now it's your turn!

Write the notes in the D major scale and add sharps to every
F and C.

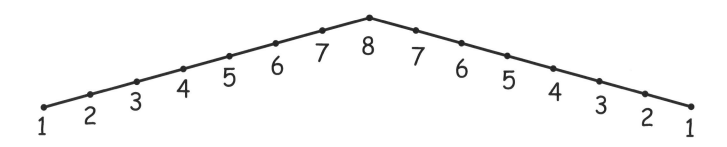

Write the D major scale using quarter notes. Start on open D
and label the sharps. Write the note names underneath.

PLAYING THE "D MAJOR" SCALE ON THE VIOLIN

Using the D major scale below, notice where the notes in the scale are on the violin.

 Notice that there are no enharmonic notes in this scale!

> The numbers on top of the notes are the fingers you could use to play the scale.

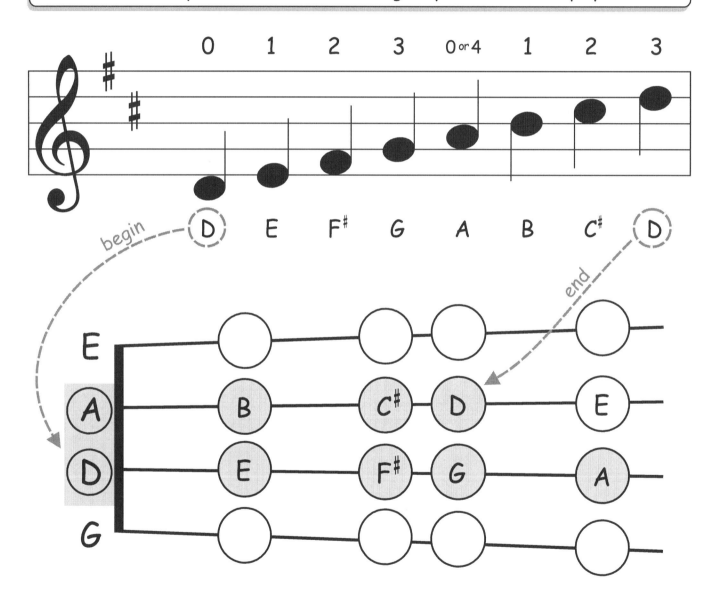

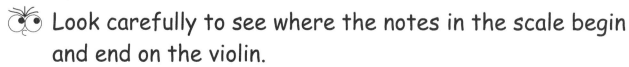 Look carefully to see where the notes in the scale begin and end on the violin.

Now its your turn. Use the music staff below to write the
D major scale.

Using the scale above, fill in the appropriate note names on the
violin diagram.

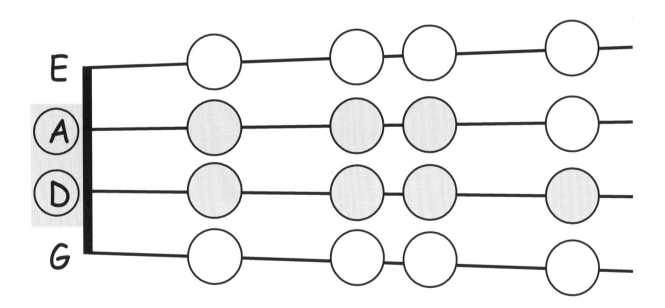

Challenging Question:
Were there any enharmonic notes in the D major scale above?

Yes or No

If so, what were they? _____

Fill in the appropriate note names on the violin diagram.

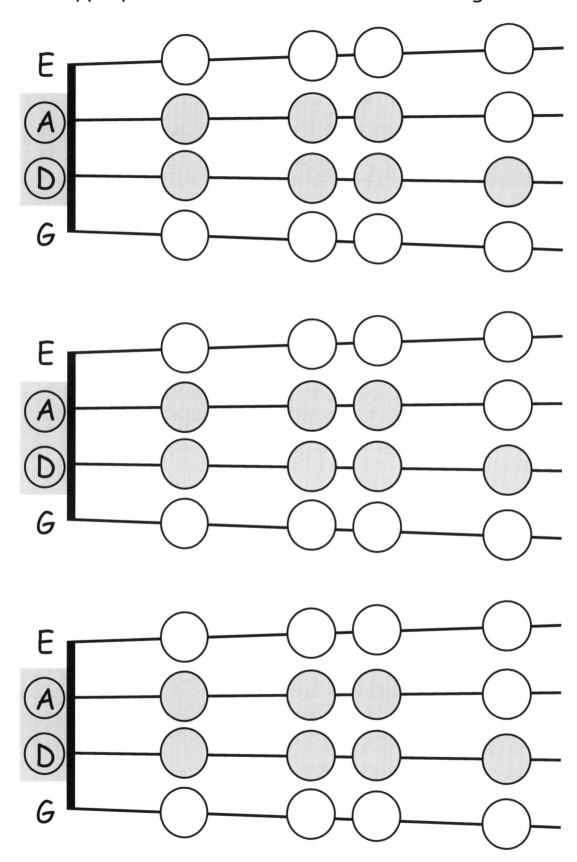

"G" MAJOR SCALE (2 PARTS)

The third scale we'll cover is the G MAJOR SCALE

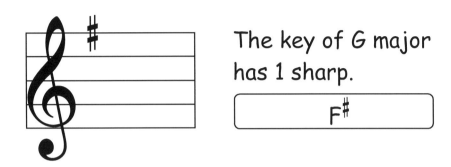

The key of G major
has 1 sharp.

F#

To write the G major scale, begin with the first letter of the
key signature and count up 8 notes.

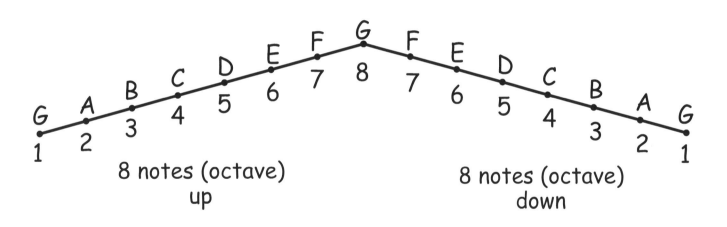

8 notes (octave)
up

8 notes (octave)
down

Now add a sharp to every F.

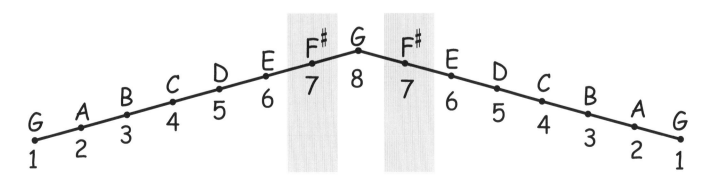

Part 1 of 2

When you write a scale on the music staff, you use the same technique you learned on the previous page.

Start on G and draw 8 notes up and 8 notes down.

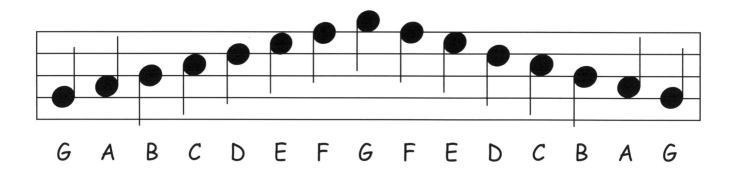

G A B C D E F G F E D C B A G

Now add a sharp to every F. Remember, the sharps are always put before the music note - not after.

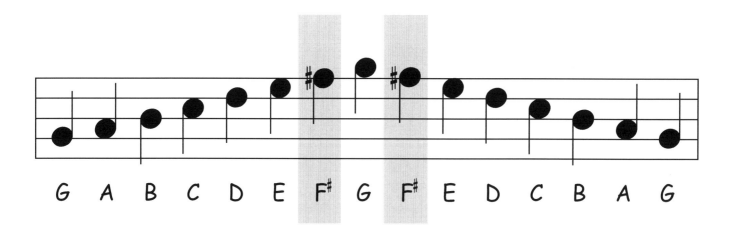

G A B C D E F# G F# E D C B A G

Now it's your turn!

Write the notes in the G major scale and add a sharp to every F.

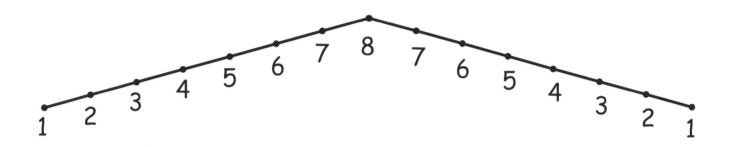

Write the G major scale using quarter notes. Start on G and label the sharp. Write the note names underneath.

PLAYING THE "G" MAJOR SCALE ON THE VIOLIN

Using the G major scale below, notice where the notes in the scale are on the violin. Notice that there are two enharmonic notes in this scale - C♮ and G♮.

The numbers on top of the notes are the fingers you could use to play the scale.

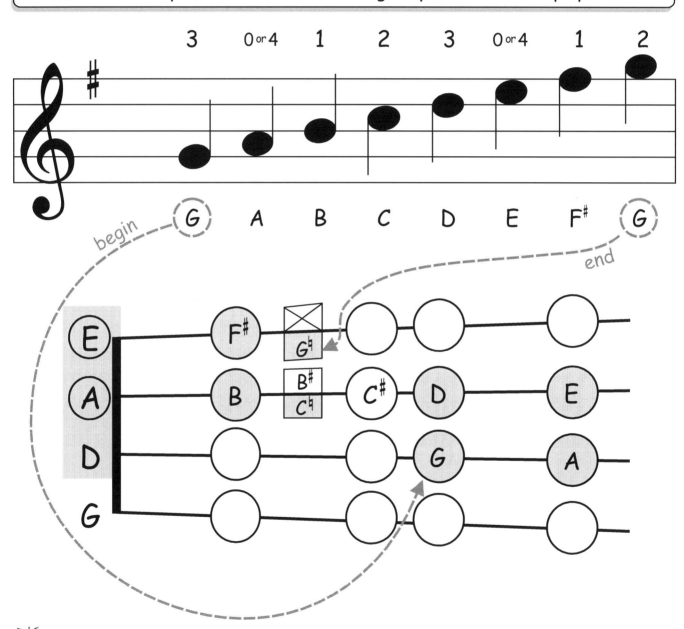

👀 Look carefully to see where the notes in the scale begin and end on the violin.

Use the music staff below to write the G major scale.

Using the scale above, fill in the appropriate note names on the violin diagram.

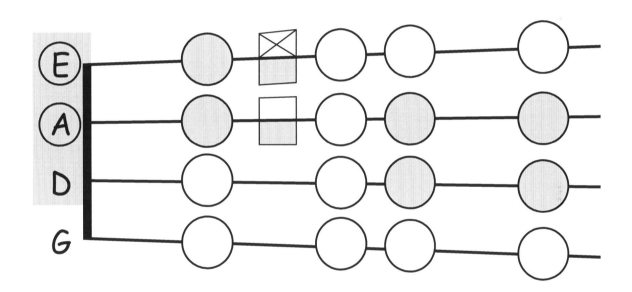

Challenging Question:
Were there any enharmonic notes in the G major scale above?

Yes or No

If so, what were they? _____

Fill in the appropriate note names on the violin diagram.

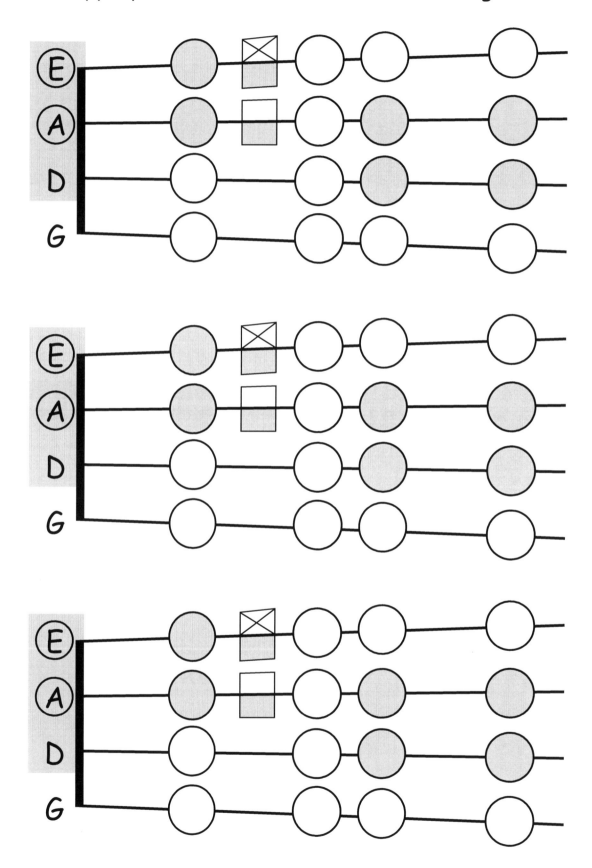

Part 2 of 2

When you write a scale on the music staff, you use the same technique you learned on the previous page.

Start on open G and draw 8 notes up and 8 notes down.

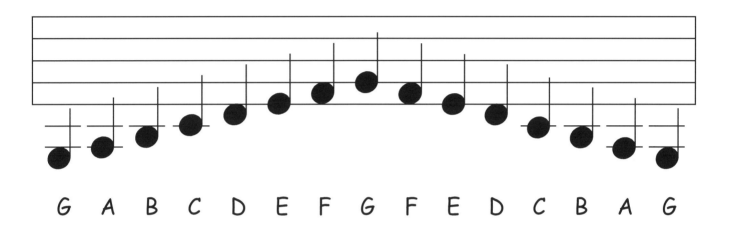

G A B C D E F G F E D C B A G

Now add a sharp to every F. Remember, the sharps are always put before the music note - not after.

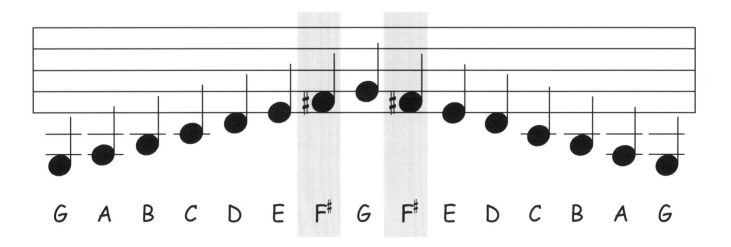

G A B C D E F# G F# E D C B A G

Now it's your turn!

Write the notes in the G major scale and add a sharp to every F.

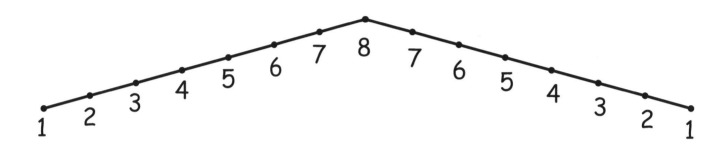

Write the G major scale using quarter notes. Start on G and label the sharp. Write the note names underneath.

PLAYING THE "G" MAJOR SCALE ON THE VIOLIN

Using the G major scale below, notice where the notes in the scale are on the violin. Notice that there are no enharmonic notes in this scale!

The numbers on top of the notes are the fingers you could use to play the scale.

👀 Look carefully to see where the notes in the scale begin and end on the violin.

Use the music staff below to write the G major scale.

Using the scale above, fill in the appropriate note names on the violin diagram.

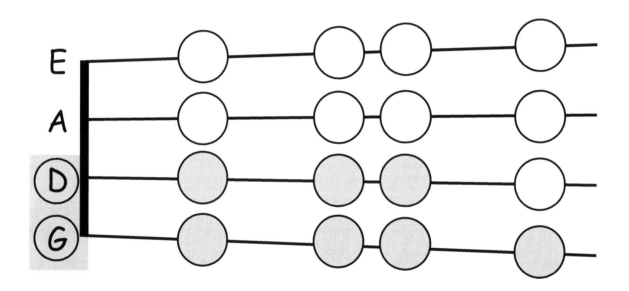

Challenging Question:
Were there any enharmonic notes in the G major scale above?

Yes or No

If so, what were they? _____

Fill in the appropriate note names on the violin diagram.

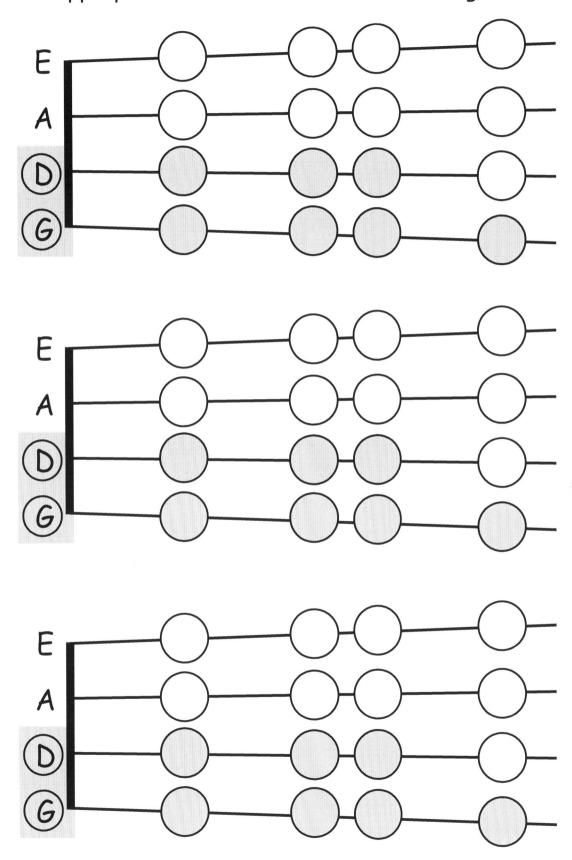

"C MAJOR" SCALE

The fourth scale we'll cover is the **C MAJOR SCALE**

The key of C major
has zero sharps.

To write the C major scale, begin with the first letter of the key signature and count up 8 notes.

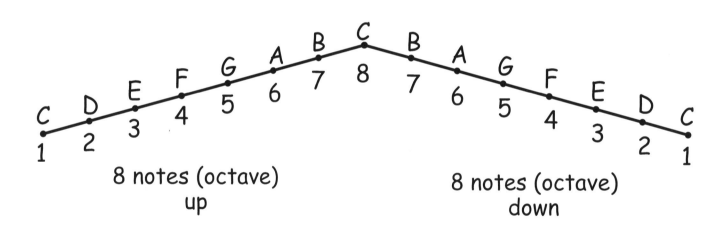

8 notes (octave)
up

8 notes (octave)
down

Since there are no sharps, the scale will stay the same.

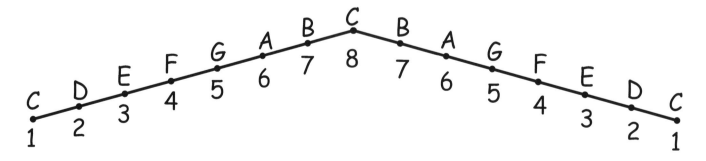

When you write a scale on the music staff, you use the same technique you learned on the previous page.

Start on the low C and draw 8 notes up and 8 notes down.

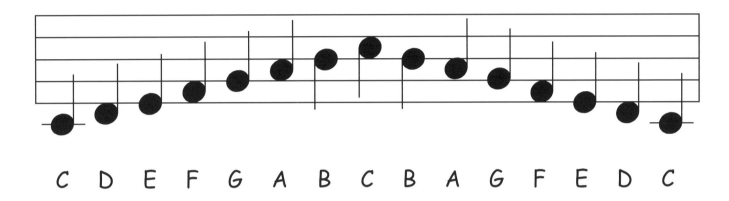

C   D   E   F   G   A   B   C   B   A   G   F   E   D   C

Since there are no sharps, the music stays exactly the same!

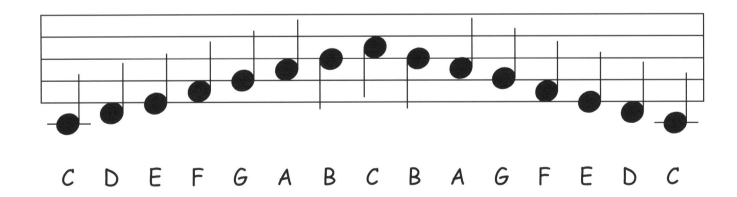

C   D   E   F   G   A   B   C   B   A   G   F   E   D   C

 Now it's your turn!

Write the notes in the C major scale.

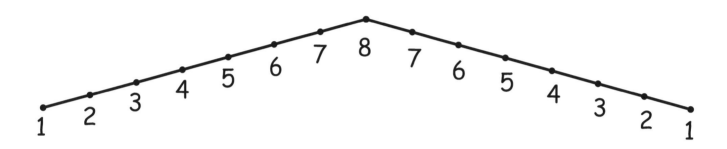

Write the C major scale using quarter notes. Start on the low C. Write the note names underneath.

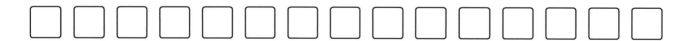

PLAYING THE "C MAJOR" SCALE ON THE VIOLIN

Using the C major scale below, notice where the notes in the scale are on the violin. Notice that there are two enharmonic notes in this scale - F♮ and C♮.

The numbers on top of the notes are the fingers you could use to play the scale.

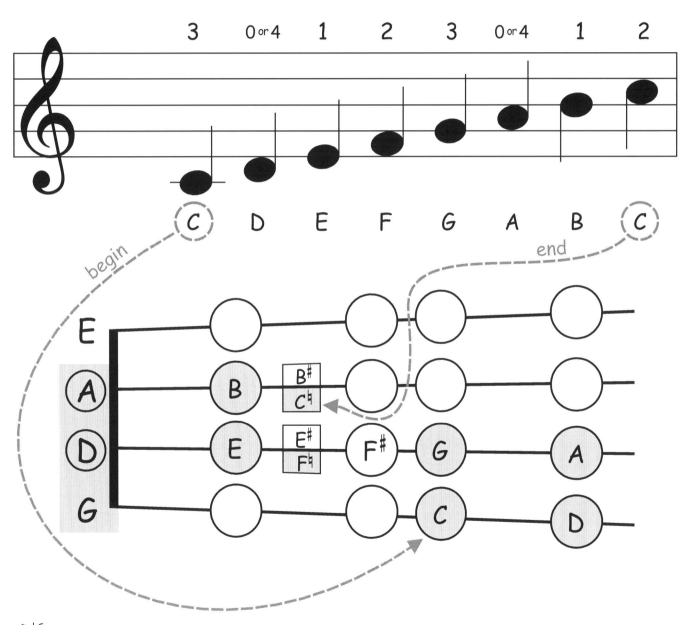

Look carefully to see where the notes in the scale begin and end on the violin.

Use the music staff below to write the C major scale.

Using the scale above, fill in the appropriate note names on the violin diagram.

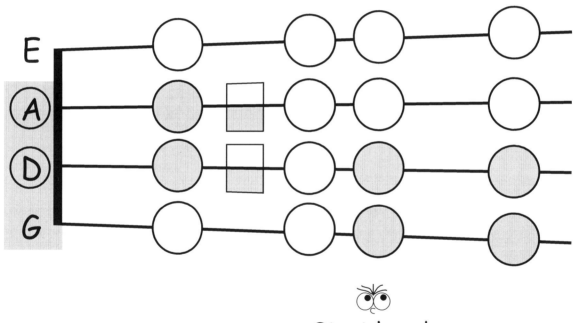

Start here!

Challenging Question:
Were there any enharmonic notes in the C major scale above?

Yes or No

If so, what were they? _____

Fill in the appropriate note names on the violin diagram.

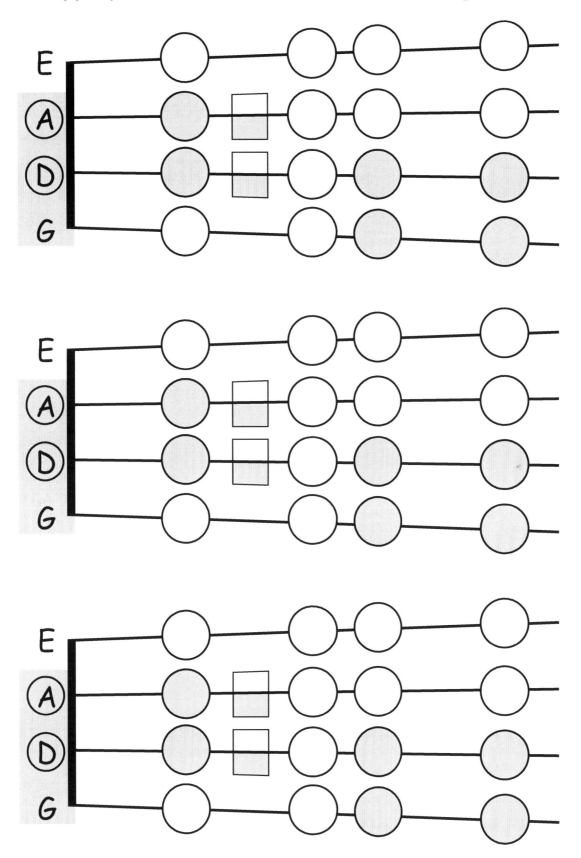

"F MAJOR" SCALE

The fifth scale we'll cover is the **F MAJOR SCALE**

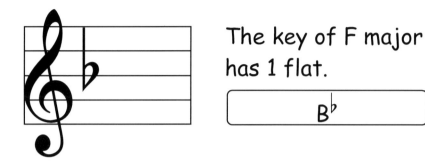

The key of F major has 1 flat.

$B\flat$

To write the F major scale, begin with the first letter of the key signature and count up 8 notes.

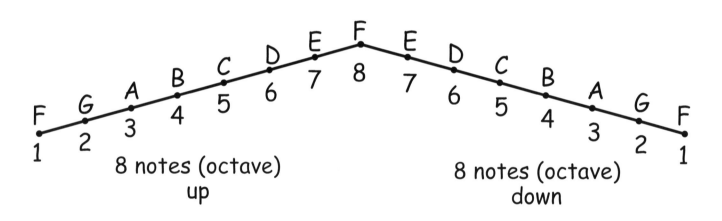

8 notes (octave) up

8 notes (octave) down

Now add a flat to every B.

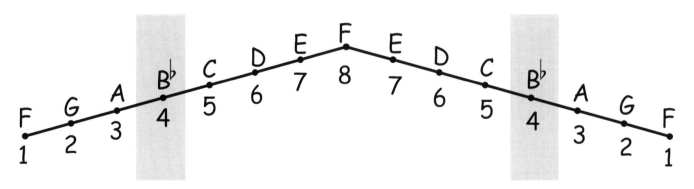

When you write a scale on the music staff, you use the same technique you learned on the previous page.

Start on the F and draw 8 notes up and 8 notes down.

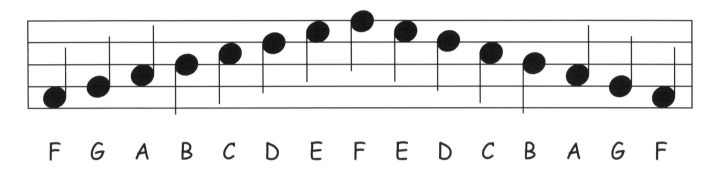

F G A B C D E F E D C B A G F

Now add a flat to every B. Remember, the flats are always put before the music note - not after.

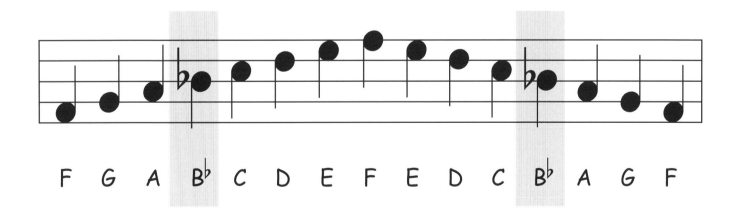

F G A B♭ C D E F E D C B♭ A G F

 Now it's your turn!

Write the notes in the F major scale and add a flat to every B.

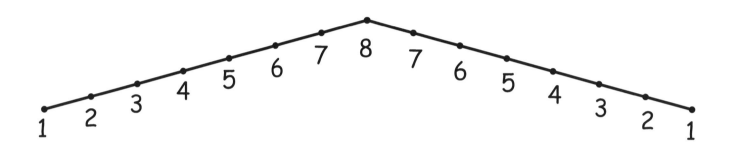

Write the F major scale using quarter notes. Start on the F and label the flat. Write the note names underneath.

PLAYING THE "F MAJOR" SCALE ON THE VIOLIN

Using the F major scale below, notice where the notes in the scale are on the violin. Notice that there are three enharmonic notes in this scale - F♮, C♮ and B♭.

The numbers on top of the notes are the fingers you could use to play the scale.

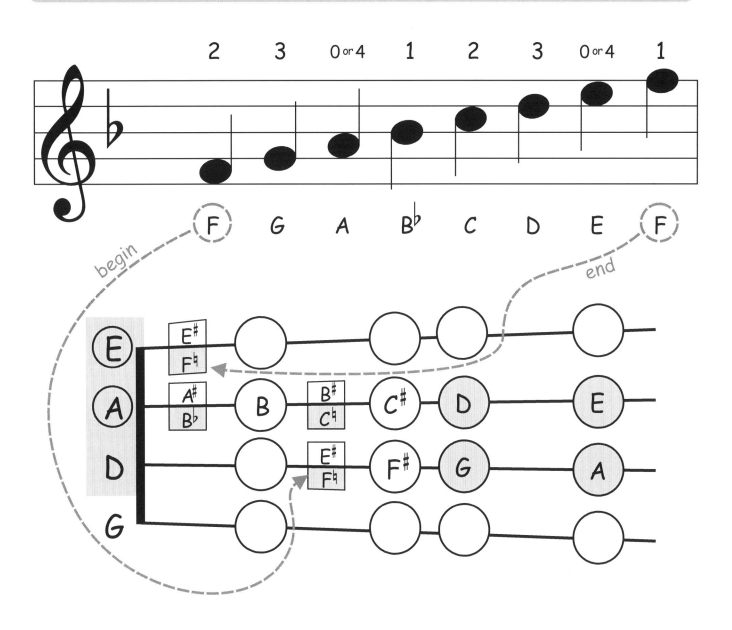

Look carefully to see where the notes in the scale begin and end on the violin.

Use the music staff below to write the F major scale.

Using the scale above, fill in the appropriate note names on the violin diagram.

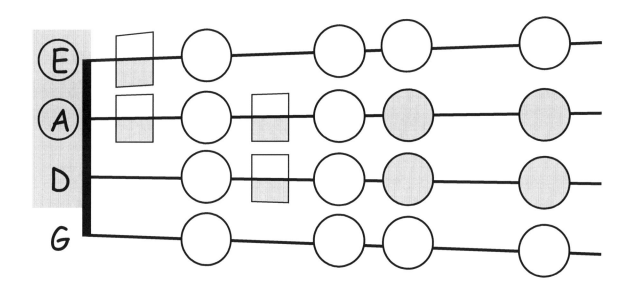

Challenging Question:
Were there any enharmonic notes in the F major scale above?

Yes or No

If so, what were they? _____

Fill in the appropriate note names on the violin diagram.

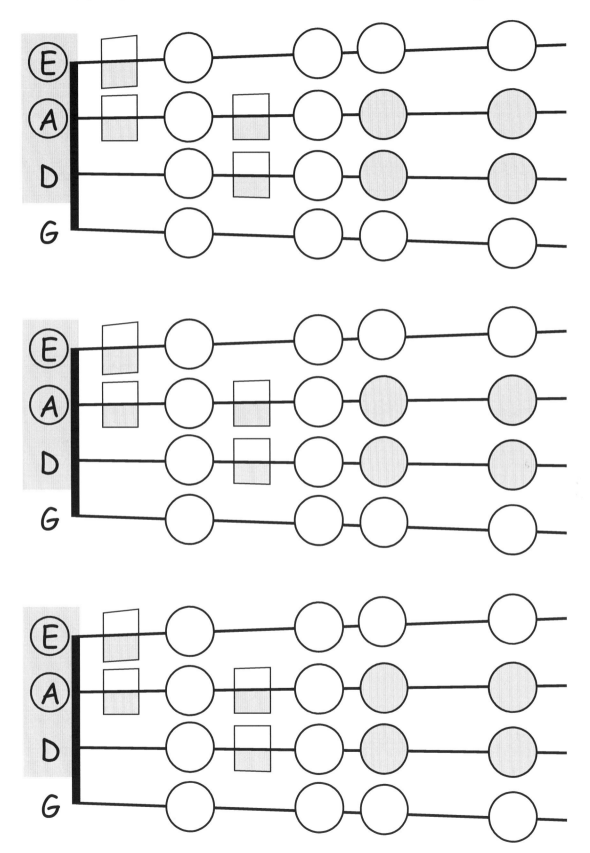

113

"B♭ MAJOR" SCALE (2 PARTS)

The sixth scale we'll cover is the **B♭ MAJOR SCALE**

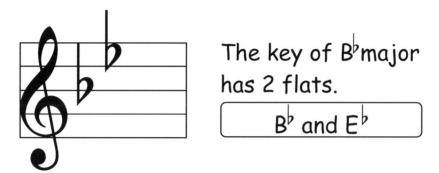

The key of B♭ major
has 2 flats.

B♭ and E♭

To write the B♭ major scale, begin with the first letter of the
key signature and count up 8 notes.

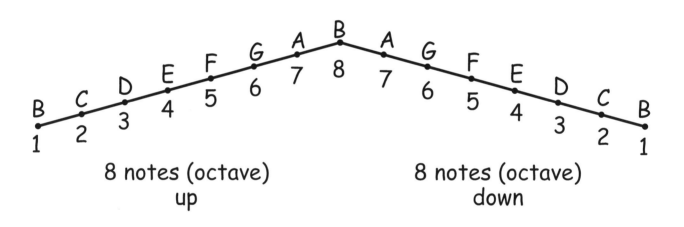

8 notes (octave)
up

8 notes (octave)
down

Now add flats to every B and E.

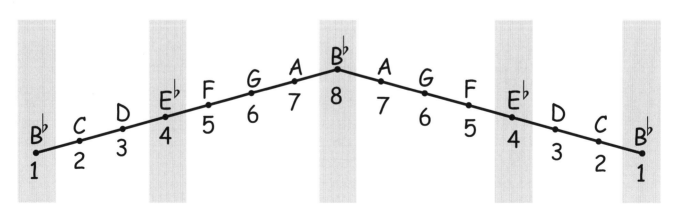

When you write a scale on the music staff, you use the same technique you learned on the previous page.

Start on the B and draw 8 notes up and 8 notes down.

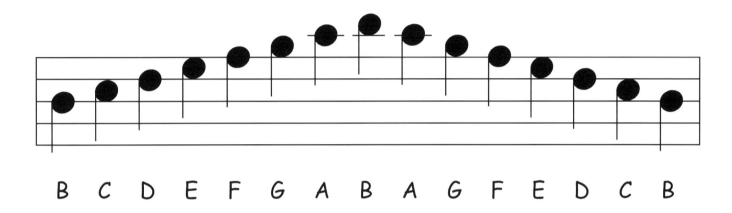

B C D E F G A B A G F E D C B

Now add flats to every B and E. Remember, the flats are always put before the music note - not after.

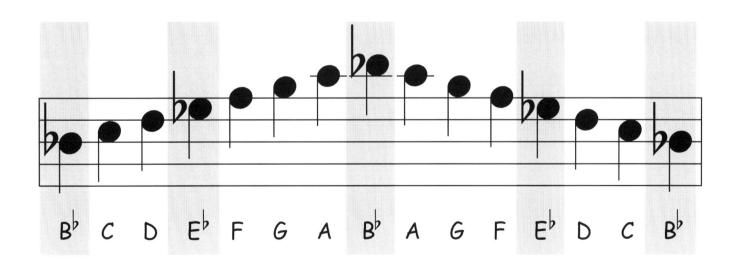

B♭ C D E♭ F G A B♭ A G F E♭ D C B♭

 Now it's your turn!

Write the notes in the B♭ major scale and add flats to every B and E.

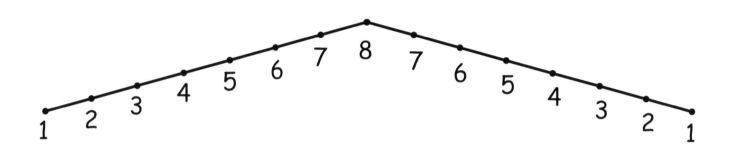

Write the B♭ major scale using quarter notes. Start on the B and label the flats. Write the note names underneath.

PLAYING THE "B♭ MAJOR" SCALE ON THE VIOLIN

Using the B♭ major scale below, notice where the notes in the scale are on the violin. Notice that there are five enharmonic notes in this scale - B♭, C♮, E♭, F♮, and G♮.

The numbers on top of the notes are the fingers you could use to play the scale.

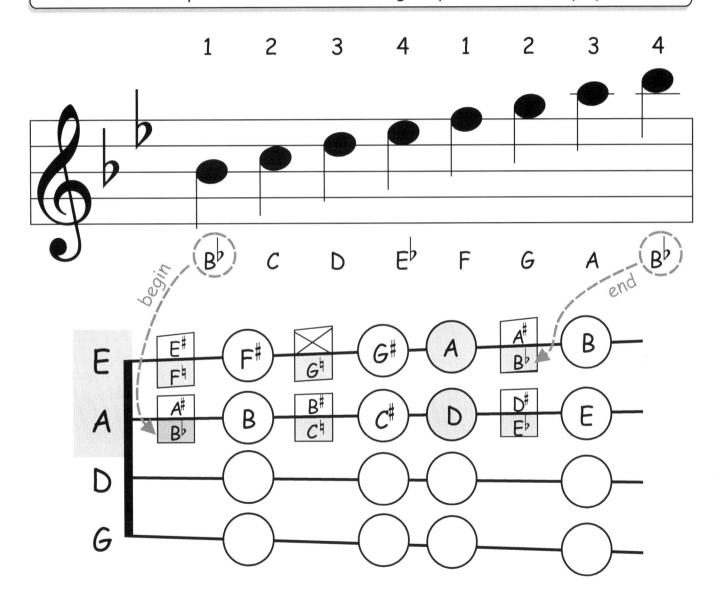

👀 Look carefully to see where the notes in the scale begin and end on the violin.

Use the music staff below to write the B♭ major scale.

Using the scale above, fill in the appropriate note names on the violin diagram.

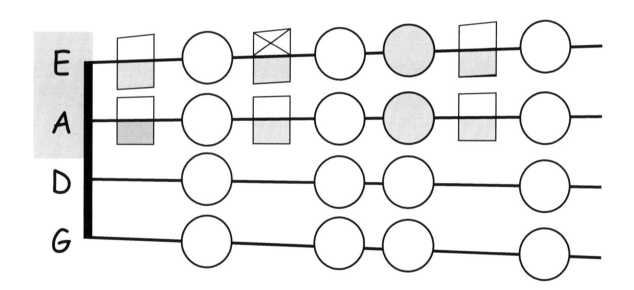

Challenging Question:
Were there any enharmonic notes in the B♭ major scale above?

Yes or No

If so, what were they? _____

118

Fill in the appropriate note names on the violin diagram.

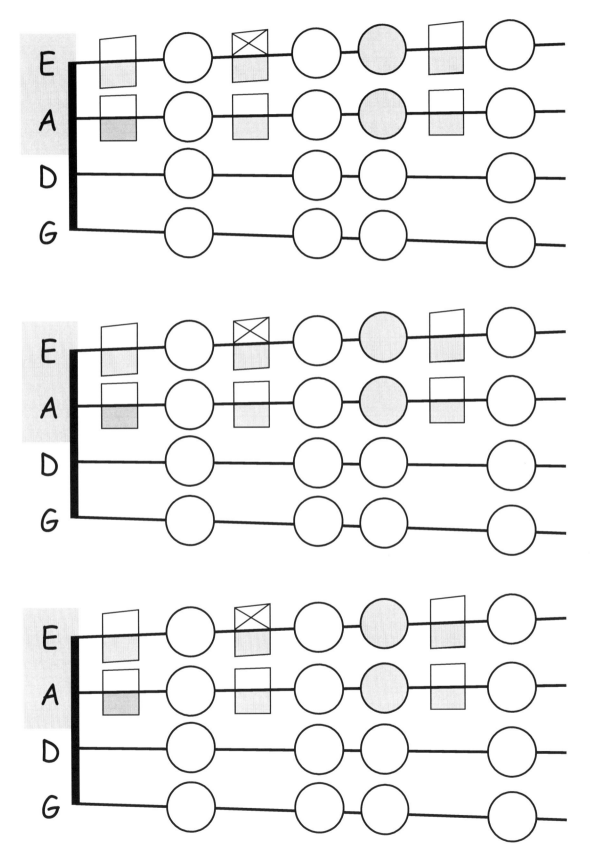

119

When you write a scale on the music staff, you use the same technique you learned on the previous page.

Start on the low B and draw 8 notes up and 8 notes down.

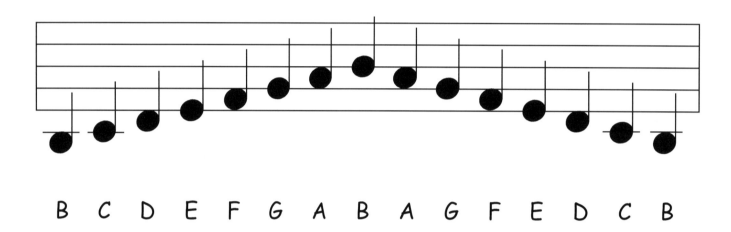

B C D E F G A B A G F E D C B

Now add flats to every B and E. Remember, the flats are always put before the music note - not after.

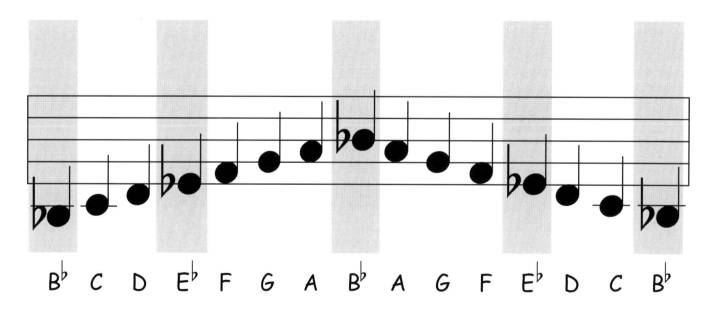

B♭ C D E♭ F G A B♭ A G F E♭ D C B♭

Now it's your turn!

Write the notes in the B♭ major scale and add flats to every B and E.

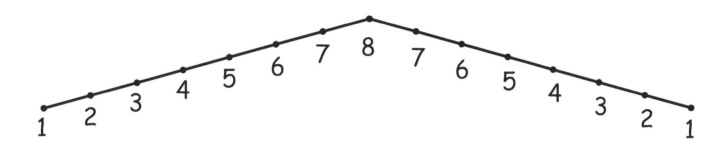

Write the B♭ major scale using quarter notes. Start on the low B and label the flats. Write the note names underneath.

PLAYING THE "B♭ MAJOR" SCALE ON THE VIOLIN

Using the B♭ major scale below, notice where the notes in the scale are on the violin. Notice that there are four enharmonic notes in this scale - B♭, E♭, F♮, and G♮.

The numbers on top of the notes are the fingers you could use to play the scale.

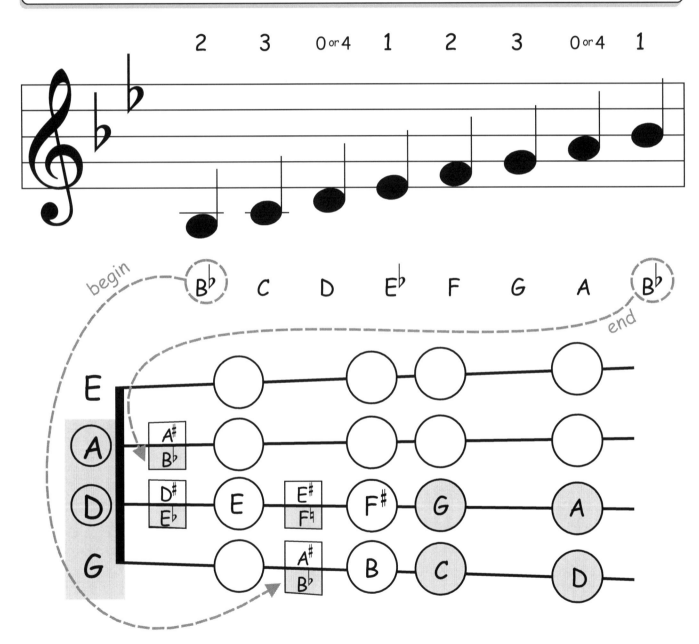

👀 Look carefully to see where the notes in the scale begin and end on the violin.

Use the music staff below to write the B♭ major scale.

Using the scale above, fill in the appropriate note names on the violin diagram.

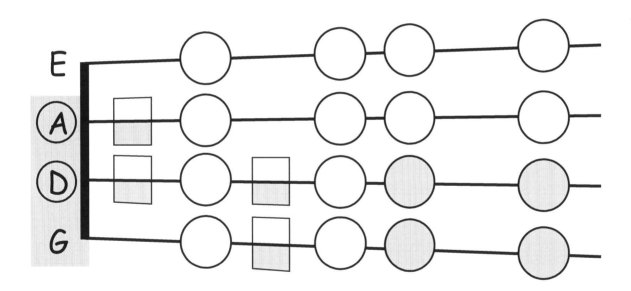

Challenging Question:
Were there any enharmonic notes in the B♭ major scale above?

Yes or No

If so, what were they? _____

Fill in the appropriate note names on the violin diagram.

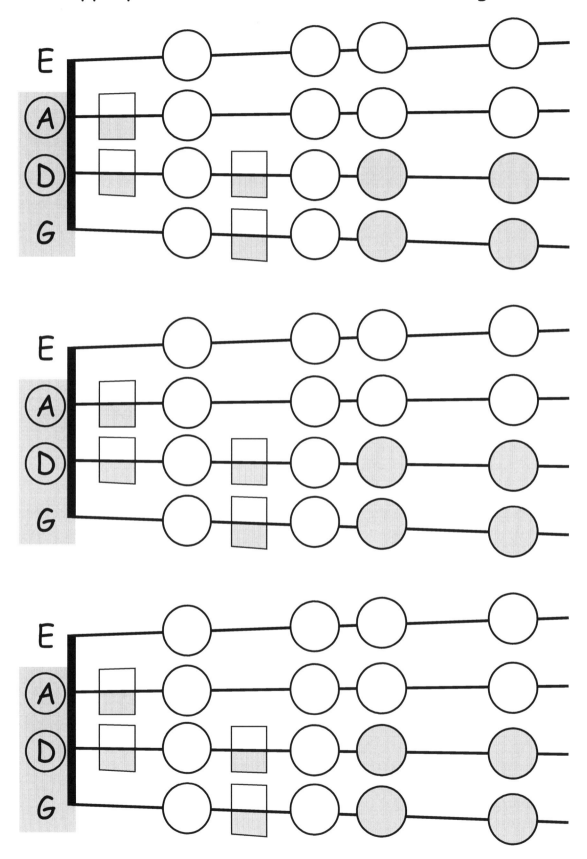

"E♭ MAJOR" SCALE

The seventh scale we'll cover is the E♭ MAJOR SCALE

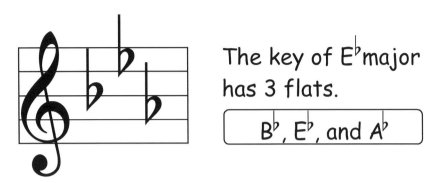

The key of E♭ major
has 3 flats.

B♭, E♭, and A♭

To write the E♭ major scale, begin with the first letter of the key signature and count up 8 notes.

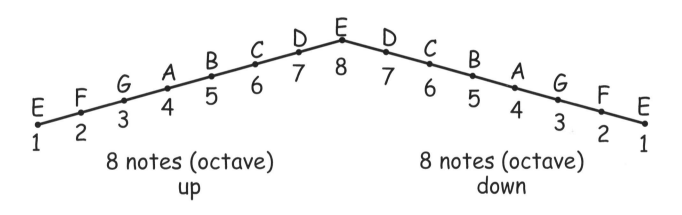

8 notes (octave)
up

8 notes (octave)
down

Now add flats to every B, E and A.

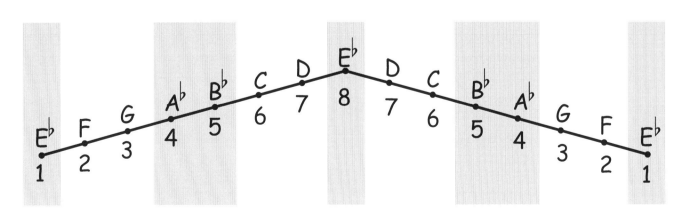

When you write a scale on the music staff, you use the same technique you learned on the previous page.

Start on the E and draw 8 notes up and 8 notes down.

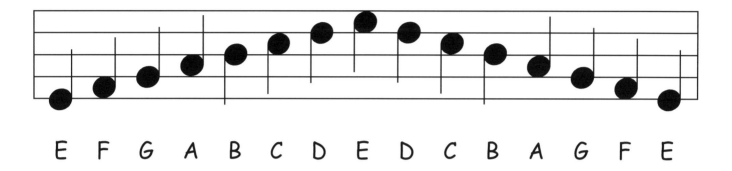

E F G A B C D E D C B A G F E

Now add flats to every B, E and A. Remember, the flats are always put before the music note - not after.

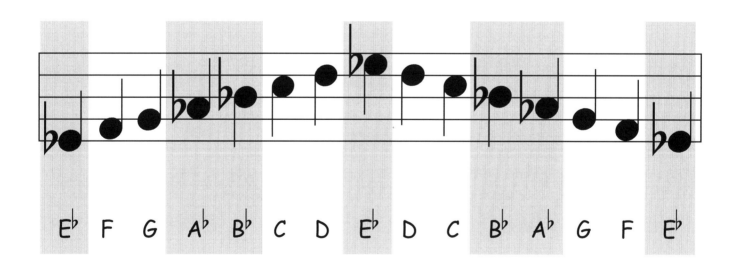

E♭ F G A♭ B♭ C D E♭ D C B♭ A♭ G F E♭

 Now it's your turn!

Write the notes in the E♭ major scale and add flats to every B, E, and A.

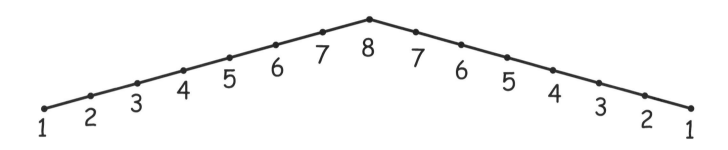

Write the E♭ major scale using quarter notes. Start on the E and label the flats. Write the note names underneath.

PLAYING THE "E♭ MAJOR" SCALE ON THE VIOLIN

Using the E♭ major scale below, notice where the notes in the scale are on the violin. Notice that there are five enharmonic notes in this scale - E♭, F♮, A♭, B♭, and C♮.

The numbers on top of the notes are the fingers you could use to play the scale.

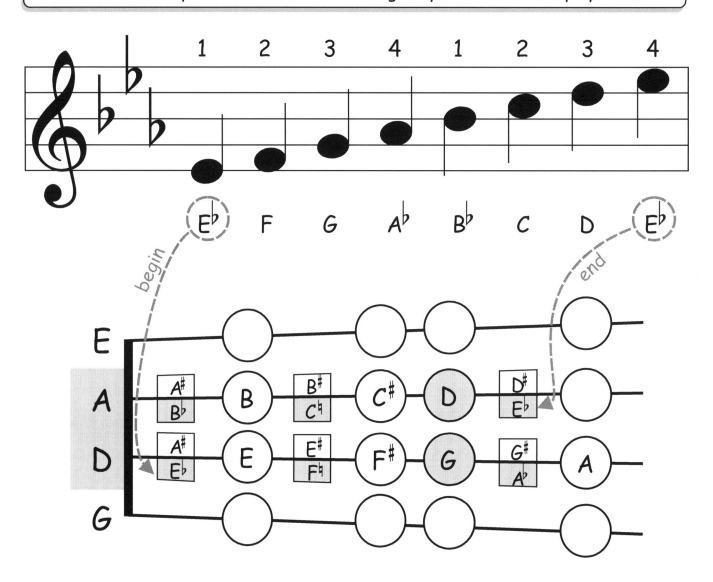

👀 Look carefully to see where the notes in the scale begin and end on the violin.

Use the music staff below to write the E♭ major scale.

Using the scale above, fill in the appropriate note names on the violin diagram.

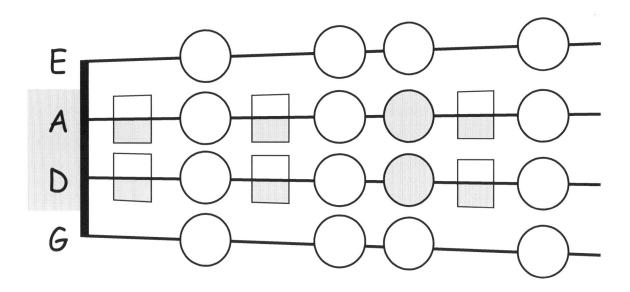

Challenging Question:
Were there any enharmonic notes in the E♭ major scale above?

Yes or No

If so, what were they? _____

Fill in the appropriate note names on the violin diagram.

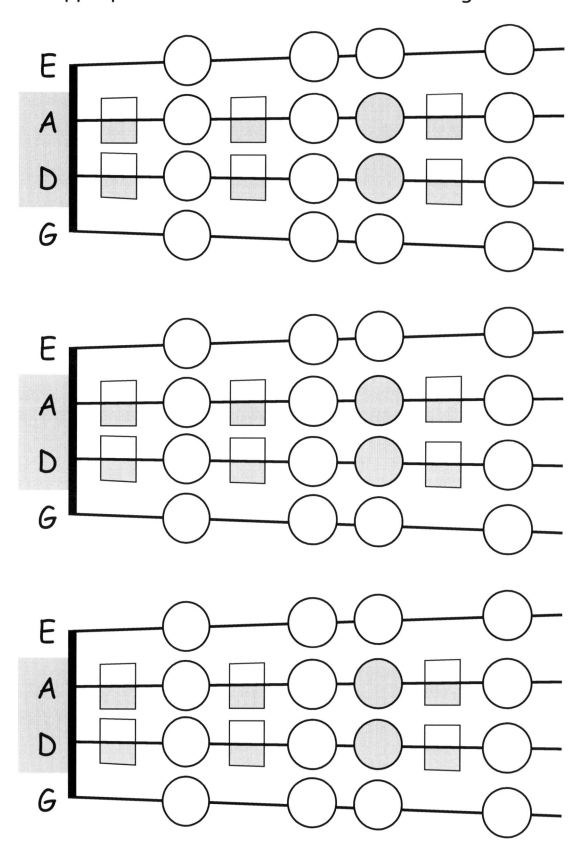

SCALE REVIEW

Draw the following scales using quarter notes. Don't forget to include the correct sharps or flats, and write the note names underneath. Using this scale, fill in the appropriate note names on the violin diagram.

A major scale (part 1)

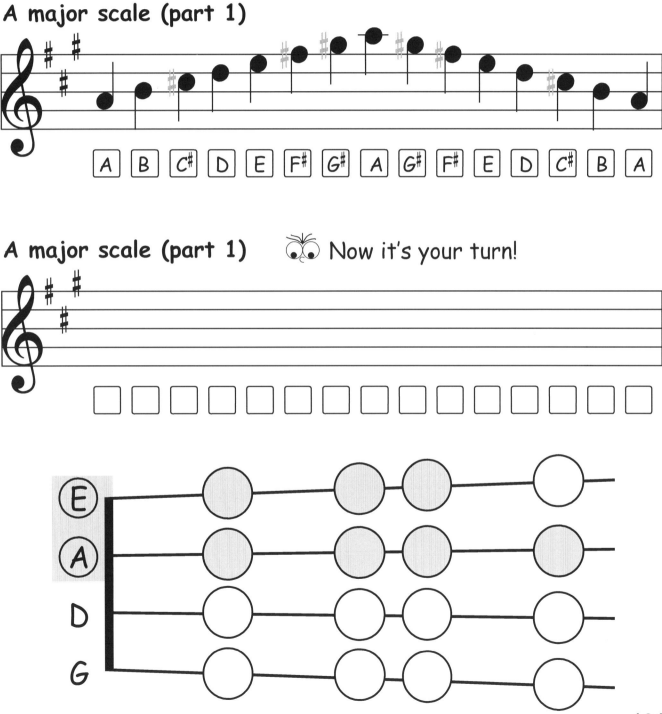

A B C♯ D E F♯ G♯ A G♯ F♯ E D C♯ B A

A major scale (part 1)   Now it's your turn!

131

A major scale (part 2)

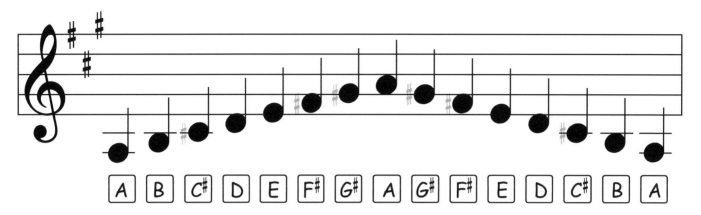

A B C♯ D E F♯ G♯ A G♯ F♯ E D C♯ B A

A major scale (part 2) Now it's your turn!

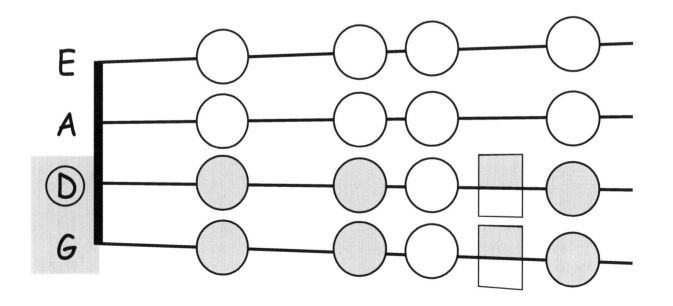

D major scale

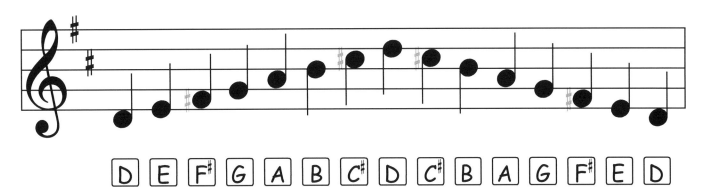

D E F# G A B C# D C# B A G F# E D

D major scale

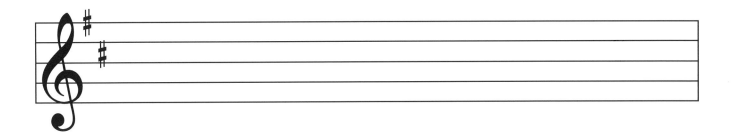

Now it's your turn!

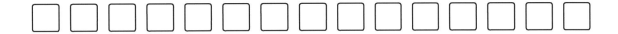

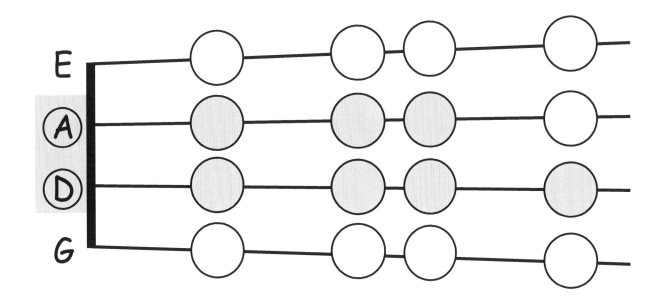

G major scale (part 1 of 2)

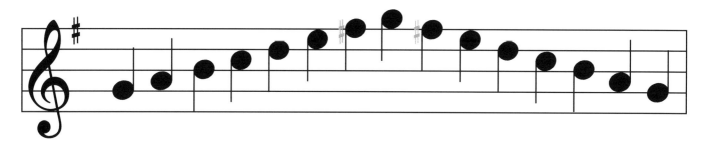

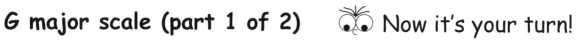

G A B C D E F# G F# E D C B A G

G major scale (part 1 of 2)   👀 Now it's your turn!

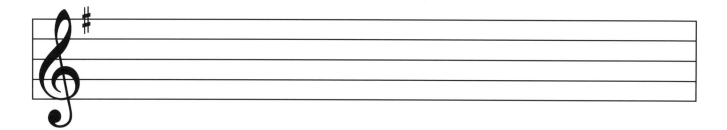

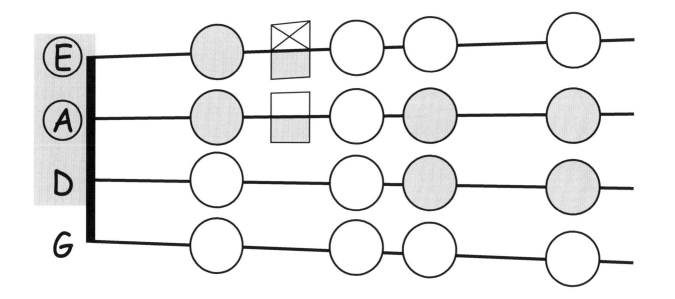

G major scale (part 2 of 2)

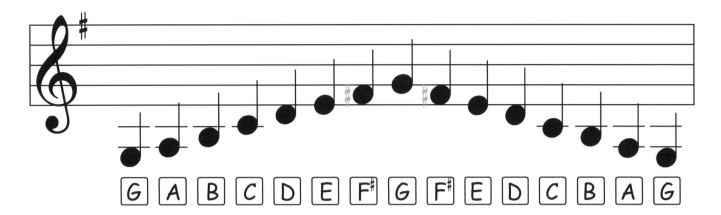

| G | A | B | C | D | E | F# | G | F# | E | D | C | B | A | G |

G major scale (part 2 of 2) 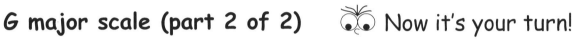 Now it's your turn!

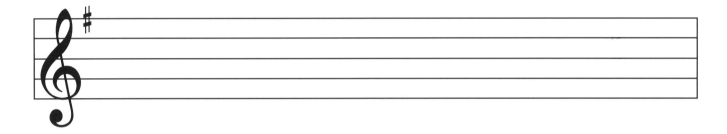

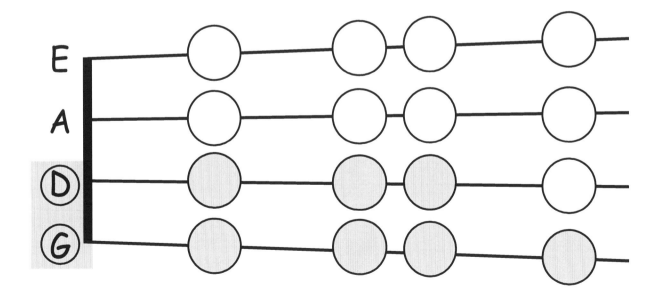

C major scale

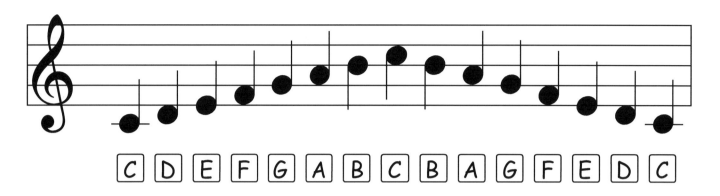

C D E F G A B C B A G F E D C

C major scale

Now it's your turn!

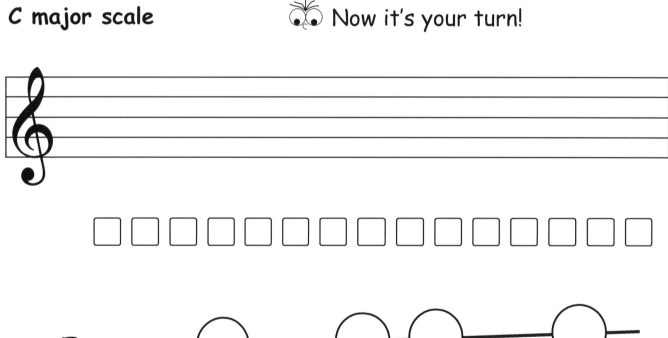

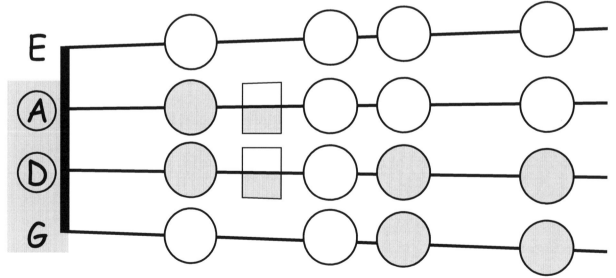

E

A

D

G

136

F major scale

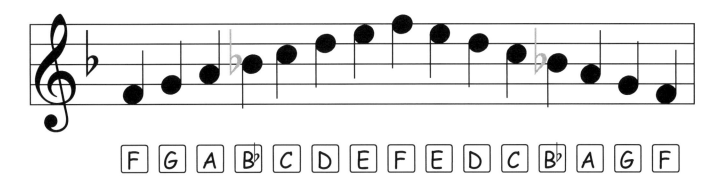

F major scale

👀 Now it's your turn!

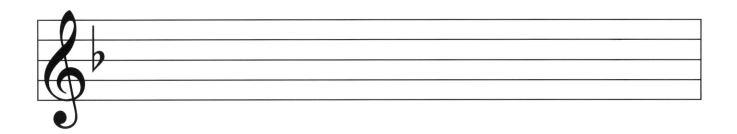

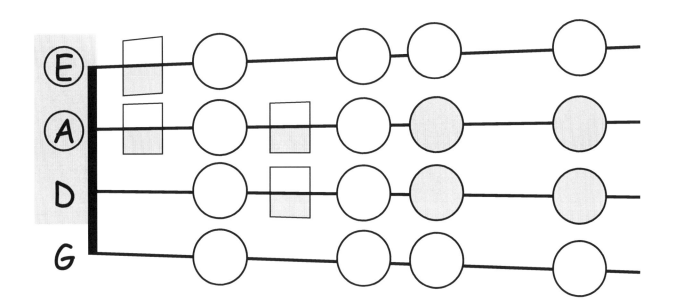

B♭ major scale (part 1 of 2)

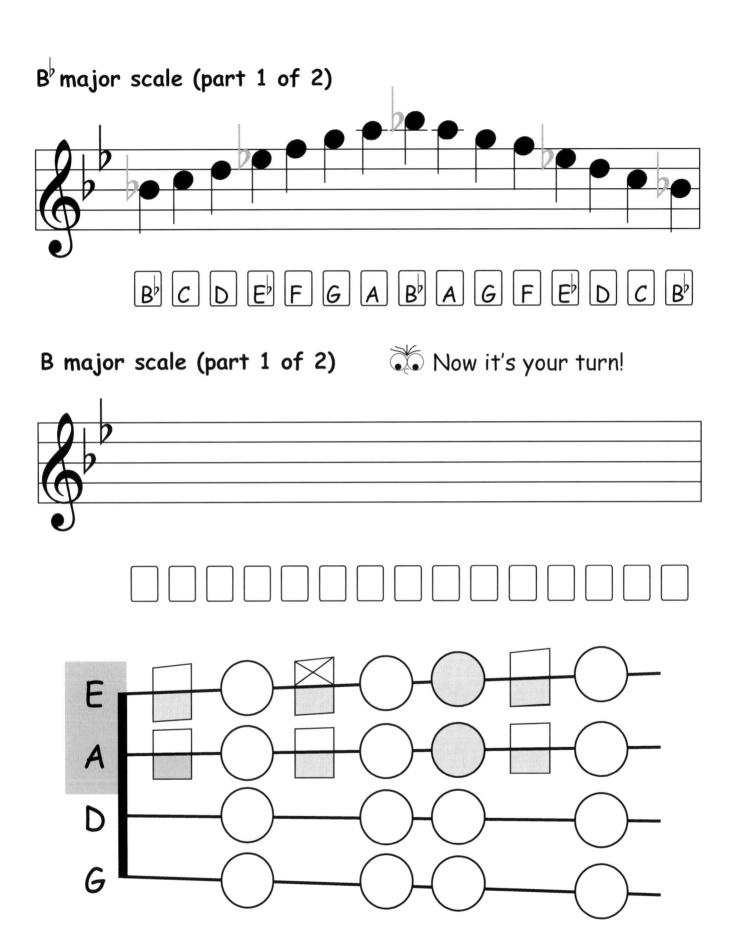

| B♭ | C | D | E♭ | F | G | A | B♭ | A | G | F | E♭ | D | C | B♭ |

B major scale (part 1 of 2)   Now it's your turn!

B♭ major scale (part 2 of 2)

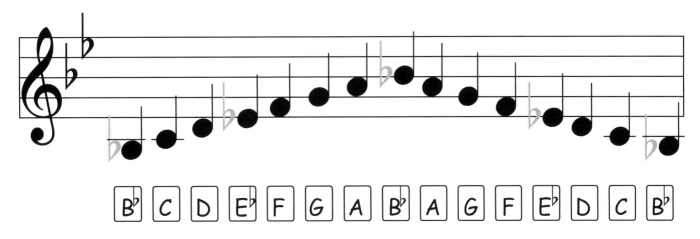

| B♭ | C | D | E♭ | F | G | A | B♭ | A | G | F | E♭ | D | C | B♭ |

B major scale (part 2 of 2) 👀 Now it's your turn!

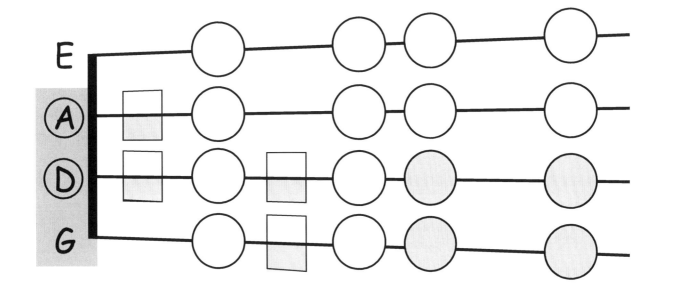

E
(A)
(D)
G

E♭ major scale

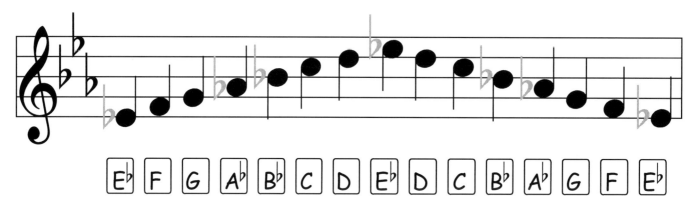

| E♭ | F | G | A♭ | B♭ | C | D | E♭ | D | C | B♭ | A♭ | G | F | E♭ |

E♭ major scale

Now it's your turn!

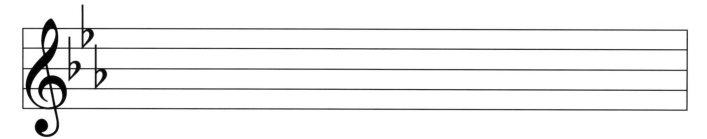

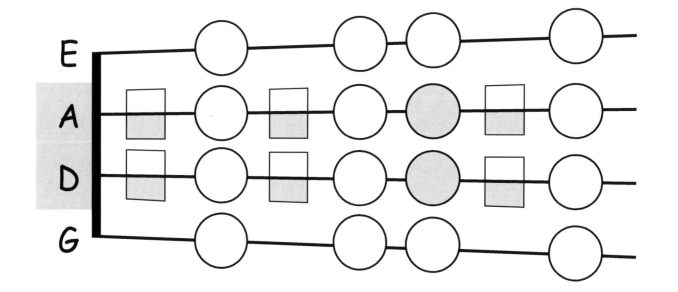

SCALE QUESTIONS

Which scale has 3 sharps? _____ The sharps are? _____

Which scale has 2 sharps? _____ The sharps are? _____

Which scale has 1 sharps? _____ The sharp is? _____

Which scale has 1 flat? _____ The flat is? _____

Which scale has 2 flats? _____ The flats are? _____

Which scale has 3 flats? _____ The flats are? _____

Which scale has 0 sharps?_____

Challenging Questions:

Where do you write key signatures in music?

_____

_____

Where do you draw sharps in music - before or after the notes?

_____

141

MUSICAL TERMS AND SYMBOLS

To play violin, there are some musical terms and signs that you must know. Here are a few of them.

(crescendo symbol)	crescendo	gradually louder
(decrescendo symbol)	decrescendo	gradually softer
(fermata symbol)	fermata	hold the note or rest longer
(tie symbol)	tie	connects 2 notes of the same pitch
(slur symbol)	slur	connects 2 notes of a different pitch
♭	flat	lowers the note a semitone or a half step
♯	sharp	raises the note a semitone or a half step
♮	natural sign	cancels out a sharp and flat
(bar line symbol)	bar line	vertical line separating the staff into measures
:‖	repeat sign	go back to the beginning and play again
p	piano	play softly
f	forte	play loudly

· (staccato mark)	staccato	short and detached note
mp	mezzopiano	medium or moderately soft
mf	mezzoforte	medium or moderately loud
𝄞	treble clef	at the beginning of each line of music
⊓	down bow	move your bow from the frog to the tip in a downward motion
∨	up bow	move your bow from the tip to the frog in a upward motion
ff	fortissimo	very loud
pp	pianissimo	very soft
rit.	ritardando	gradually slow down
(music staff)	music staff	the lines and spaces where the music notes are written

FINDING MUSICAL TERMS & SYMBOLS IN MUSIC

Exercise 1a

Circle the following musical signs in the box below. Be careful, there are more signs than you will need to use. Choose carefully.

Staccato note, treble clef, key signature, ritardando, time signature.

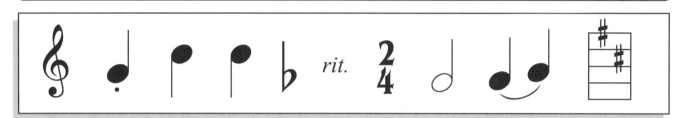

Exercise 1b

1. Circle the staccato notes in yellow.
2. Circle the treble clefs in orange.
3. Circle the key signatures in blue.
4. Circle the ritardando in green.
5. Circle the time signature in purple.

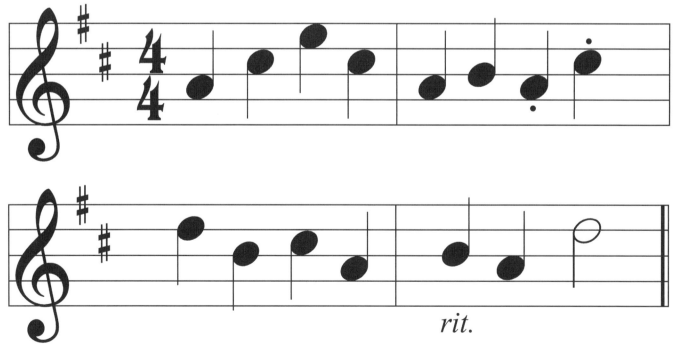

144

Exercise 2a

Circle the following musical signs in the box below. Be careful, there are more signs than you will need to use. Choose carefully.

> quarter note, double bar line, staccato note, slur, down bow.

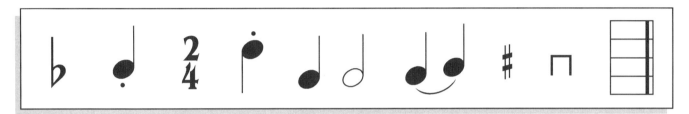

Exercise 2b

1. Color the quarter notes in red.
2. Color the double bar line in pink.
3. Color the staccato notes in purple.
4. Color the slurs in blue.
5. Color the down bow in green.

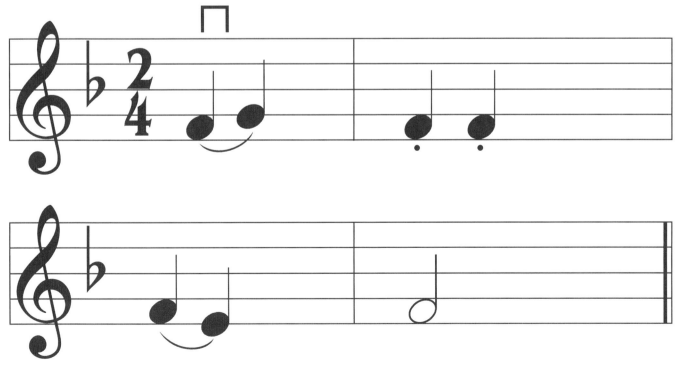

Exercise 3a

Circle the following musical signs in the box below. Be careful, there are more signs than you will need to use. Choose carefully.

half note, treble clef, time signature, forte, bar line.

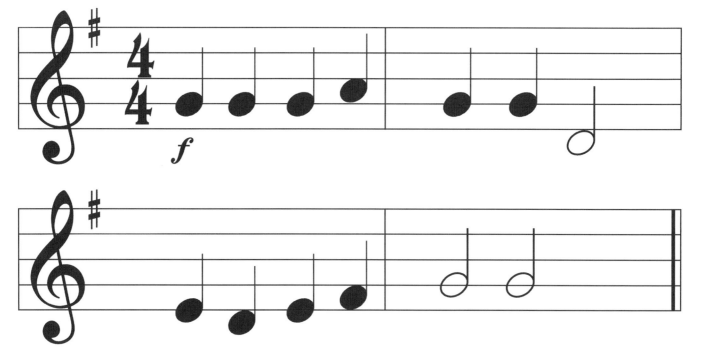

Exercise 3b

1. Color the half notes in orange.
2. Color the treble clefs in green.
3. Color the time signature in red.
4. Color the forte in yellow.
5. Color the bar lines in blue.

Exercise 4a

Circle the following musical signs in the box below. Be careful, there are more signs than you will need to use. Choose carefully.

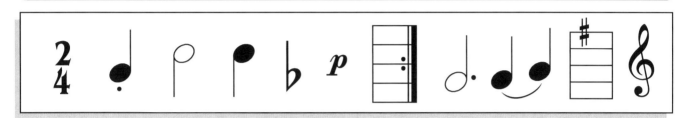

Exercise 4b

1. Color the dotted half notes in purple.
2. Color the key signatures in blue.
3. Color the repeat sign in yellow.
4. Color the piano in pink.
5. Color the treble clefs in green.

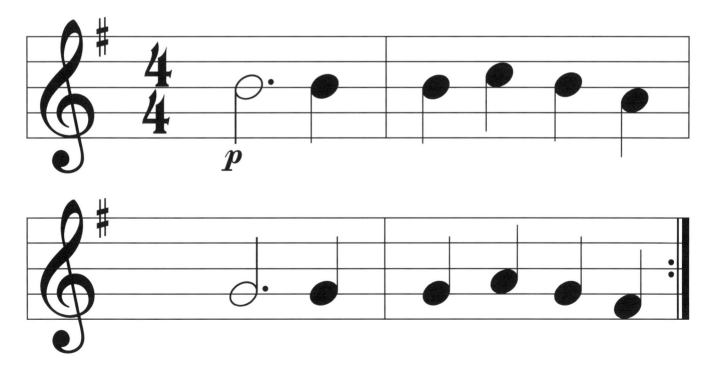

BOOK REVIEW

What is the order of sharps? Draw them and write letters underneath.

What is the order of flats? Draw them and write letters underneath.

Make up your own music using a treble clef, D major key signature, $\frac{3}{4}$ time signature, any combination of notes or rests and a bar line.

Make up your own music using a treble clef, A major key signature, $\frac{4}{4}$ time signature, any combination of notes or rests and a bar line.

148

Draw the 17 notes you know on the violin using quarter notes and circle where the stem changes. Remember one note can have a stem that goes either up or down.

Draw the A major scale using quarter notes. Don't forget to add a treble clef and key signature.

Draw the E♭ major scale using quarter notes. Don't forget to add a treble clef and key signature.

Draw the C major scale using whole notes. Don't forget to add a treble clef and key signature.

What is an enharmonic?

_____

_____

What is different about one of the enharmonic pairs on the
E string?

_____

_____

Where is the treble clef located in music?

_____

What does the key signature do?

_____

_____

What does the time signature do?

_____

_____

What music symbol tells you to hold the note longer?

What music symbol tells you to play softly?

What music symbol tells you to move your bow from
    tip to frog?

What symbol tells you to play very loud?

150

Certificate
of Accomplishment

This certifies that

_____

has successfully completed Book Three

Beginner Violin Theory
for Children workbook

_____
Teacher

_____
Date

Appendix - Answer Key Page 51

Do these notes go higher or lower? Fill in the blanks.

♭ → ♮ → ♯   ♯ → ♮ → ♭
(higher)   (lower)

1. ♯ → ♮   _____lower_____

2. ♭ → ♮   _____higher_____

3. ♯ → ♮   _____lower_____

4. ♮ → ♭   _____lower_____

5. ♯ → ♮   _____lower_____

6. ♭ → ♮   _____higher_____

7. ♯ → ♮   _____lower_____

8. ♮ → ♭   _____lower_____

9. ♯ → ♮   _____lower_____

10. ♭ → ♮   _____higher_____

11. ♮ → ♭   _____lower_____

12. ♯ → ♮   _____lower_____

Appendix - Answer Key Page 55

What are the 4 enharmonics pairs you can play with your 1st finger?

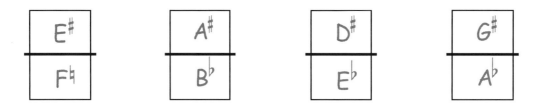

E♯	A♯	D♯	G♯
F♮	B♭	E♭	A♭

Which note is higher? Circle the higher note. If the notes are the same, circle both. Use the diagram to help you.

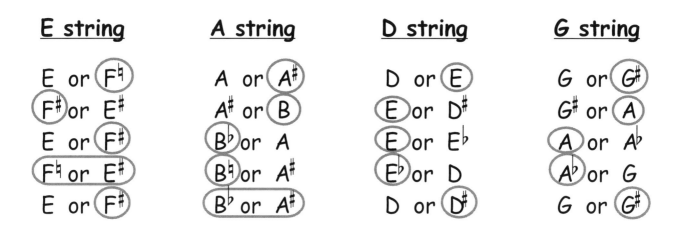

E string

E or (F♮)
(F♯) or E♯
E or (F♯)
(F♮ or E♯)
E or (F♯)

A string

A or (A♯)
A♯ or (B)
(B♭) or A
(B♮ or A♯)
(B♭ or A♯)

D string

D or (E)
(E) or D♯
(E) or E♭
(E♭) or D
D or (D♯)

G string

G or (G♯)
G♯ or (A)
(A) or A♭
(A♭) or G
G or (G♯)

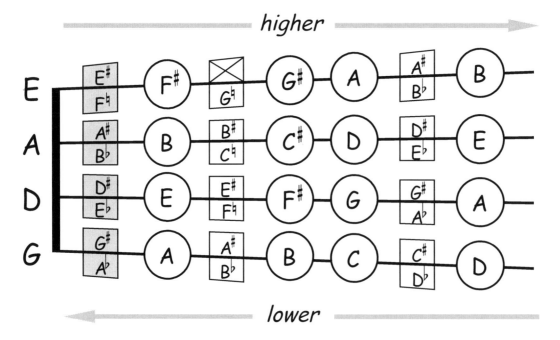

higher

lower

Appendix - Answer Key Page 56

Which note is lower? Circle the lower note. If the notes are the same, circle both. Use the diagram to help you.

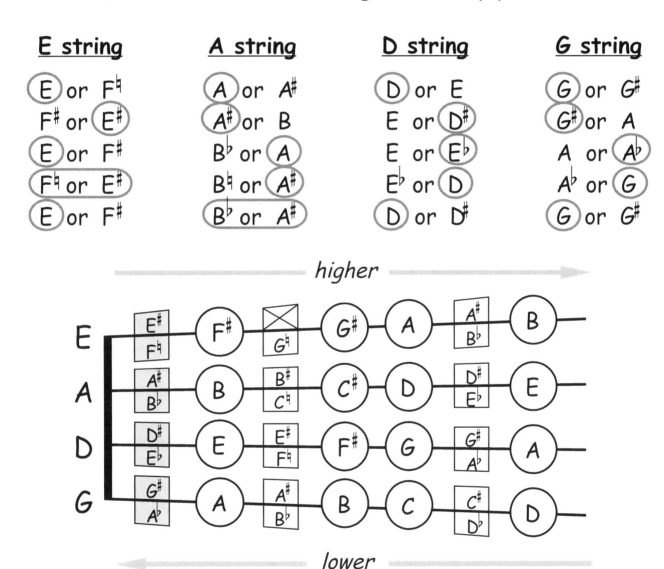

E string
- (E) or F♮
- F♯ or (E♯)
- (E) or F♯
- (F♮ or E♯)
- (E) or F♯

A string
- (A) or A♯
- (A♯) or B
- B♭ or (A)
- B♮ or (A♯)
- (B♭ or A♯)

D string
- (D) or E
- E or (D♯)
- E or (E♭)
- E♭ or (D)
- (D) or D♯

G string
- (G) or G♯
- (G♯) or A
- A or (A♭)
- A♭ or (G)
- (G) or G♯

higher ➡

E — E♯ / F♮ — F♯ — ⊠ / G♮ — G♯ — A — A♯ / B♭ — B

A — A♯ / B♭ — B — B♯ / C♮ — C♯ — D — D♯ / E♭ — E

D — D♯ / E♭ — E — E♯ / F♮ — F♯ — G — G♯ / A♭ — A

G — G♯ / A♭ — A — A♯ / B♭ — B — C — C♯ / D♭ — D

⬅ lower

Challenging Question: What is an enharmonic?

When the same note has 2 different names.

Appendix - Answer Key Page 58

What are the 4 enharmonics pairs you can play with your 1st and 2nd finger?

Which note is higher? Circle the higher note. If the notes are the same, circle both. Use the diagram to help you.

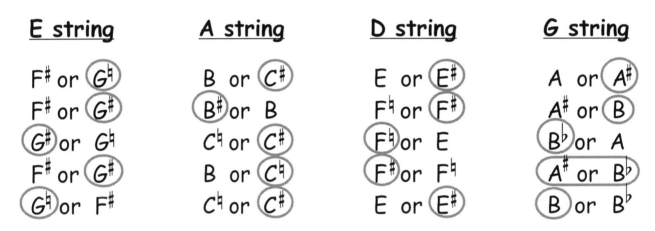

E string

F♯ or (G♮)
F♯ or (G♯)
(G♯) or G♮
F♯ or (G♯)
(G♮) or F♯

A string

B or (C♯)
(B♯) or B
C♮ or (C♯)
B or (C♮)
C♮ or (C♯)

D string

E or (E♯)
F♮ or (F♯)
(F♮) or E
(F♯) or F♮
E or (E♯)

G string

A or (A♯)
A♯ or (B)
(B♭) or A
(A♯ or B♭)
(B) or B♭

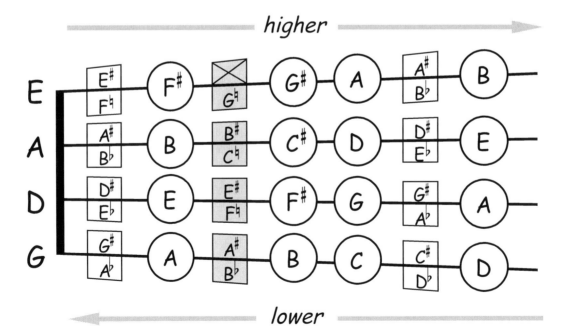

Appendix - Answer Key Page 59

Which note is lower? Circle the lower note. If the notes are the same, circle both. Use the diagram to help you.

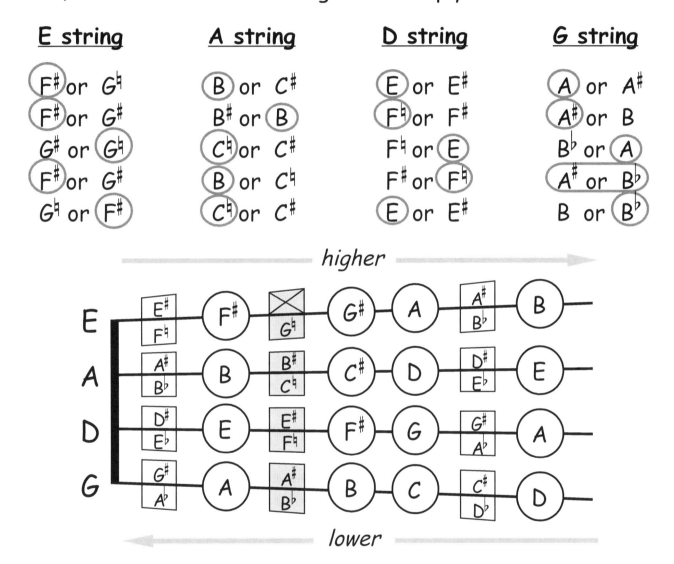

E string	A string	D string	G string
(F♯) or G♮	(B) or C♯	(E) or E♯	(A) or A♯
(F♯) or G♯	B♯ or (B)	(F♮) or F♯	(A♯) or B
G♯ or (G♮)	(C♮) or C♯	F♮ or (E)	B♭ or (A)
(F♯) or G♯	(B) or C♮	F♯ or (F♮)	(A♯ or B♭)
G♮ or (F♯)	(C♮) or C♯	(E) or E♯	B or (B♭)

Challenging Question:
What is different about the enharmonic pair on the E string?

The F♯ becomes a double sharp.

What are the 4 enharmonics pairs you can play with your 3rd and 4th finger?

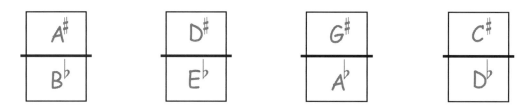

Which note is higher? Circle the higher note. If the notes are the same, circle both. Use the diagram to help you.

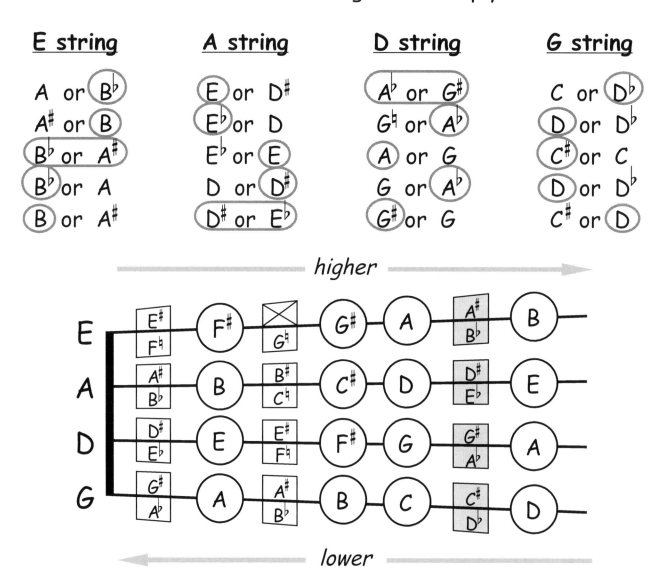

E string

A or (B♭)
A♯ or (B)
(B♭ or A♯)
(B♭) or A
(B) or A♯

A string

(E) or D♯
(E♭) or D
E♭ or (E)
D or (D♯)
(D♯ or E♭)

D string

(A♭ or G♯)
G♮ or (A♭)
A or G
G or (A♭)
(G♯) or G

G string

C or (D♭)
(D) or D♭
(C♯) or C
(D) or D♭
C♯ or (D)

Appendix - Answer Key Page 62

Which note is lower? Circle the lower note. If the notes are the same, circle both. Use the diagram to help you.

E string	A string	D string	G string
(A) or B♭	E or (D♯)	(A♭ or G♯)	(C) or D♭
(A♯) or B	E♭ or (D)	(G♮) or A♭	D or (D♭)
(B♭ or A♯)	(E♭) or E	A or (G)	C♯ or (C)
B♭ or (A)	(D) or D♯	(G) or A♭	D or (D♭)
B or (A♯)	(D♯ or E♭)	G♯ or (G)	(C♯) or D

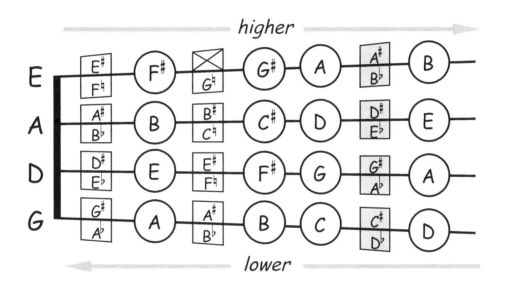

higher

lower

Challenging Question:

List all the enharmonic pairs you have learned. (Hint - there are 12 pairs)

E string	E♯ / F♮	✕ / G♮	A♯ / B♭
A string	A♯ / B♭	B♯ / C♮	D♯ / E♭
D string	D♯ / E♭	E♯ / F♮	G♯ / A♭
G string	G♯ / A♭	A♯ / B♭	C♯ / D♭

ENHARMONICS REVIEW

Fill in the following charts. Add the correct notes.

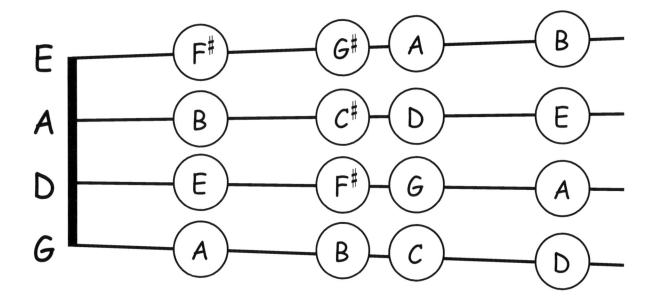

Add the correct notes and enharmonic pairs.

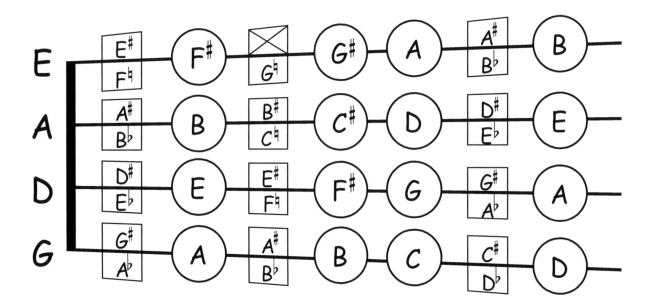

Appendix - Answer Key Page 66

Now it's your turn. Fill in the rest of the arrows on the diagram to show every chromatic semitone on the violin.
Start at the open string.

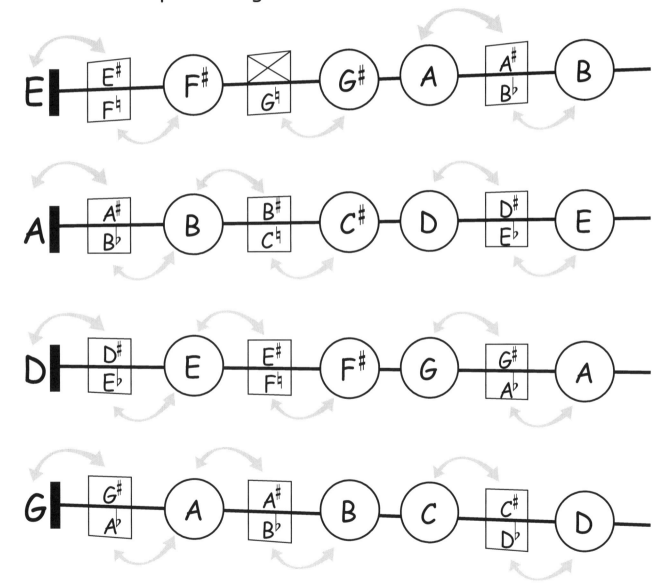

Appendix - Answer Key Page 68

Now it's your turn. Fill in the rest of the arrows on the diagram to show every diatonic semitone on the violin.
Start at the open string.

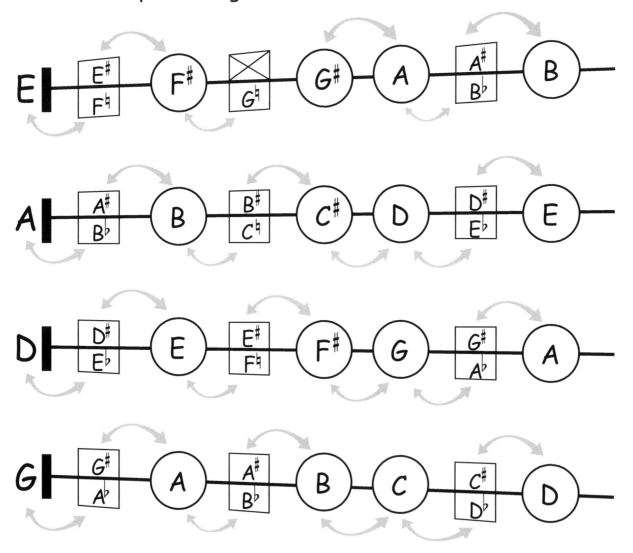

SEMITONES REVIEW

Chromatic Semitones

 Remember - you only move one half step up or down to a note with the same letter.

What is a chromatic semitone of:

F♯ ➡ F♮   D♭ ➡ D♮

G♮ ➡ G♯ OR G♭   E♮ ➡ E♭ OR E♯

A♭ ➡ A♮   F♮ ➡ F♯ OR F♭

B♮ ➡ B♯ OR B♭   G♯ ➡ G♮

C♯ ➡ C♮   A♮ ➡ A♭ OR A♯

Diatonic Semitones

 Remember - you only move one half step up or down to a note with a different letter.

What is a diatonic semitone of:

F♯ ➡ G♮ OR E♯   D♭ ➡ C♮

G♮ ➡ F♯ OR A♭   E♮ ➡ F♮ OR D♯

A♭ ➡ G♮   F♮ ➡ E♮

B♮ ➡ A♯ OR C♮   G♯ ➡ A♮

C♯ ➡ D♮ OR B♯   A♮ ➡ B♭ OR G♯

Appendix - Answer Key Page 71

Fill in the rest of the arrows on the diagram to show every wholetone on the violin. Start with each open string.

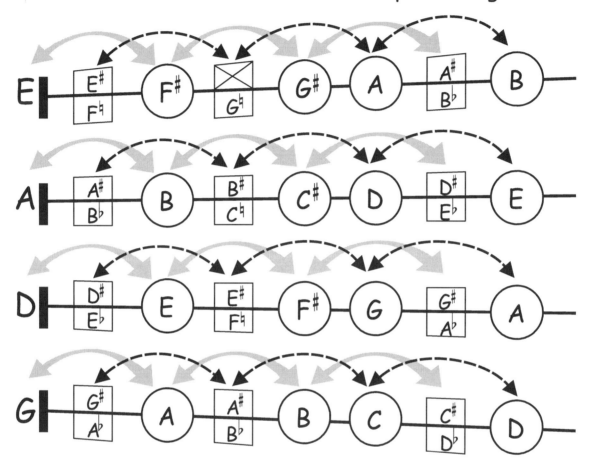

Wholetones Review

Remember - move 2 half steps up or down.

What is a wholetone of:

F♯ ➡ G♯ or E♯ or A♭   D♭ ➡ D♯ or E♭ or B♯

G♮ ➡ F♮ or A♮ or E♯   E♮ ➡ F♯ or D♮

A♭ ➡ F♯ or A♯ or B♭   F♮ ➡ G or D♯ or E♭

B♮ ➡ C♯ or D♭ or A♯   G♯ ➡ F♯ or A♯ or B♭

C♯ ➡ B♮ or D♯ or E♭   A♮ ➡ B♮ or G♮

SEMITONE AND WHOLETONES REVIEW

Use this diagram for help.

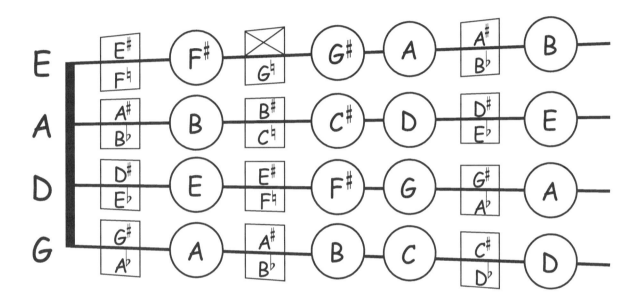

Fill in the blanks.

chromatic semitones

F♮ → F♯ OR F♭

G♯ → G♮

A♭ → A♮

B♮ → B♯ OR B♭

C♮ → C♯ OR C♭

D♭ → D♮

diatonic semitones

F♮ → E♮

G♯ → A♮

A♭ → G♮

B♮ → A♯ OR C♮

C♮ → B♮ OR D♭

D♭ → C♮

wholetones

F♮ → G♮ OR D♯ OR E♭

G♯ → A♯ OR F♯ OR B♭

A♭ → A♯ OR F♯ OR B♭

B♮ → A♮ OR C♯ OR D♭

C♮ → D♮ OR B♭ OR A♯

D♭ → B♮ OR D♯ OR E♭

FINDING MUSICAL TERMS & SYMBOLS IN MUSIC

Exercise 1a

Circle the following musical signs in the box below. Be careful, there are more signs than you will need to use. Choose carefully.

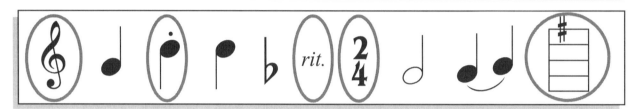

Staccato note, treble clef, key signature, ritardando, time signature.

Exercise 1b

1. Circle the staccato notes in yellow.
2. Circle the treble clefs in orange.
3. Circle the key signatures in blue.
4. Circle the ritardando in green.
5. Circle the time signature in purple.

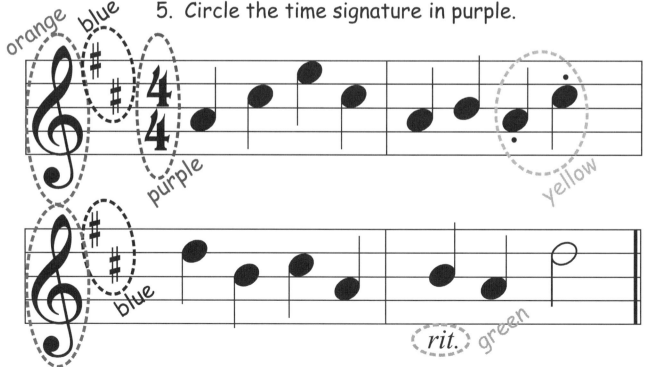

Exercise 2a

Circle the following musical signs in the box below. Be careful, there are more signs than you will need to use. Choose carefully.

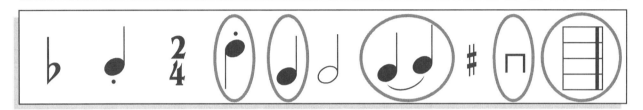

quarter note, double bar line, staccato note, slur, down bow.

Exercise 2b

1. Color the quarter notes in red.
2. Color the double bar line in pink.
3. Color the staccato notes in purple.
4. Color the slurs in blue.
5. Color the down bow in green.

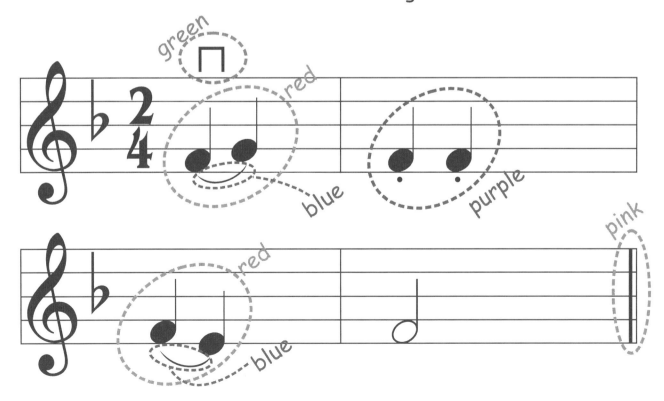

Appendix - Answer Key Page 146

Exercise 3a

Circle the following musical signs in the box below. Be careful, there are more signs than you will need to use. Choose carefully.

half note, treble clef, time signature, forte, bar line.

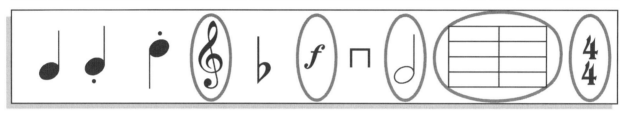

Exercise 3b

1. Color the half notes in orange.
2. Color the treble clefs in green.
3. Color the time signature in red.
4. Color the forte in yellow.
5. Color the bar lines in blue.

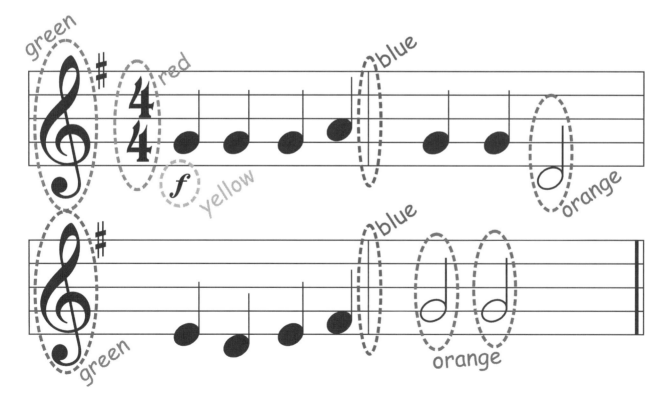

Appendix - Answer Key Page 147

Exercise 4a

Circle the following musical signs in the box below. Be careful, there are more signs than you will need to use. Choose carefully.

dotted half note, key signature, repeat sign, piano, treble clef.

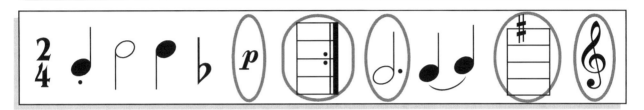

Exercise 4b

1. Color the dotted half notes in purple.
2. Color the key signatures in blue.
3. Color the repeat sign in yellow.
4. Color the piano in pink.
5. Color the treble clefs in green.

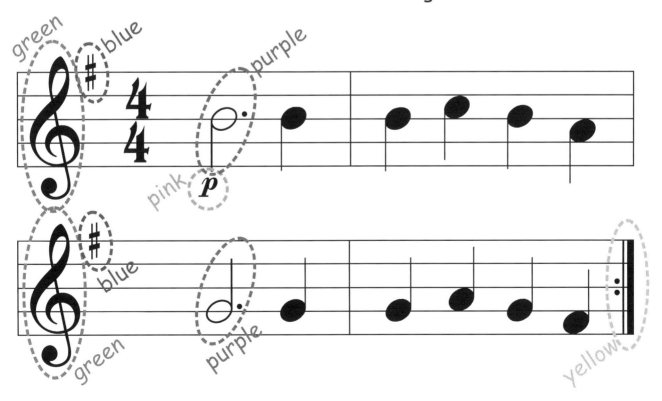

6819120R00095

Made in the USA
San Bernardino, CA
15 December 2013